Preface

Software Engineering is one of the most critical and ever-evolving fields in the realm of technology today. As the backbone of software development, it plays a pivotal role in designing, developing, testing, and maintaining software systems that power everything from business applications to mobile devices. Understanding the significance of Software Engineering, the Indira Gandhi National Open University (IGNOU) has incorporated this subject into its curriculum, offering students a comprehensive understanding of both the theoretical frameworks and practical skills needed to excel in the industry.

This book, IGNOU Software Engineering Previous Years Unsolved Papers, is a thoughtfully compiled collection of unsolved question papers from past years. It is designed to serve as an indispensable resource for students preparing for their examinations in Software Engineering. The primary aim of this book is to provide students with an effective tool to self-assess their grasp of the subject, pinpoint areas that require further study, and enhance their problem-solving abilities.

We firmly believe that one of the most effective ways to prepare for exams is by practicing with previous years' question papers. This approach not only helps students become familiar with the various types and formats of questions they may encounter but also deepens their understanding of the subject matter by encouraging the application of concepts to practical scenarios. By working through these unsolved papers, students can evaluate their readiness, refine their time management skills during exams, and gain confidence in handling complex and challenging questions.

The choice to leave the papers unsolved is deliberate. Our intention is to encourage students to actively engage with the content, think critically, and explore different methods and approaches to solving the problems presented. This approach promotes independent learning and ensures that students are better equipped to handle a variety of question formats and difficulties during their actual exams.

This book covers a broad spectrum of topics within Software Engineering, including software development life cycles, design methodologies, testing techniques, project management, and software maintenance. Each paper has been carefully chosen to ensure comprehensive coverage of the syllabus, providing students with a thorough understanding of the key concepts needed to succeed in their exams.

We hope that this book will not only support students in their academic pursuits but also inspire them to explore deeper into the field of Software Engineering. As technology continues to advance, the knowledge and skills acquired in Software Engineering will undoubtedly be instrumental in shaping the future of software development and innovation.

We would like to express our sincere appreciation to the faculty members and students of IGNOU who have contributed to the creation of this book. Your feedback and insights have been invaluable in ensuring that this book meets the needs of today's learners.

We wish you the best of luck in your studies and future endeavours in the dynamic world of Software Engineering.

Table of Contents

Master Of Computer Applications (MCA)
Chapter 1: Term-End Examination, December, 2021
MCS-213: Software Engineering

Time: 3 Hours
Maximum Marks: 100
Weightage: 70

Note: (i) Question No. 1 is compulsory.
(ii) Answer any three Questions from the rest.

1. (a) Define "Software Review". What are its types? Explain them. 10

(b) What is Data Dictionary? Explain with an example. 10

(c) List and explain various phases of Waterfall model.

(d) What is meant by "Functional Requirements"? How are they different from "Non-functional Requirements"? Give examples for them. 10

2. (a) What is Black Box Testing? How does it differ from White Box Testing? 10

(b) Explain various sections of SRS with an example. 10

3. (a) What are the steps involved in Software Project Estimation? Explain. 10

(b) What is Coupling? Explain various types of Coupling. 10

4. (a) Draw the first three levels of DFDs for a "Library Information System." Make necessary assumptions. 10

(b) Explain COCOMO model in detail. 10

5. (a) Explain any one of the Risk Management Techniques. 10

(b) Explain any five techniques for Requirement Gathering. 10

Master Of Computer Applications (MCA)
Chapter 2: Term-End Examination, June, 2022
MCS-213: Software Engineering

Time: 3 Hours
Maximum Marks: 100
Weightage: 70

Note: (i) Question No. 1 is compulsory.
(ii) Answer any three Questions from the rest.

1. (a) Define Cleanroom Software Engineering. What is its significance? Discuss the underlying principles of Cleanroom-based Software Development. 10

(b) List and explain various phases of Spiral Model. 10

(c) Write a short note on Cyclomatic Complexity. 10

(d) Explain various levels of SEI-CMM. 10

2. (a) What is Unit Testing? How does it differ from Integration Testing? 10

(b) Develop SRS for a "Railway Reservation System". Make necessary assumptions. 10

3. (a) What is meant by "Change Management"? Explain the process of Change Management. 10

(b) What is Cohesion? Explain various types of Cohesion. 10

4. (a) Draw the first 3-levels of DFD's for a "Railway Reservation System". Make necessary assumptions. 10

(b) What is meant by "Verification"? How does it differ from "Validation"? Give an example for each. 10

5. (a) What is meant by "Version Control"? Explain with an example. 10

(b) Write a short note on "Baselines". 10

MCS-213

Master Of Computer Applications (MCA)
Chapter 3: Term-End Examination, December, 2022
MCS-213: Software Engineering

Time: 3 Hours
Maximum Marks: 100
Weightage: 70

Note: (i) Question No. 1 is compulsory.
(ii) Answer any three Questions from the rest.

1. (a) What are the different methods used for estimating cost and efforts required for completing a project successfully? Explain any one of the methods. 10

(b) Explain McCall's Quality factors. 10

(c) Explain various steps involved in Debugging. 10

(d) Briefly explain the process of Software Configuration Management. 10

2. (a) Write a short note on "Human Computer Interface (HCI)". 10

(b) Develop SRS for a "Hospital Management System." Make necessary assumptions. 10

3. (a) What is Alpha Testing? How does it differ from Beta Testing? 10

(b) Define the term "Risk". Explain different phases of Risk Management. 10

4. (a) Explain any two methods for scheduling of Software Projects. 10

(b) What is meant by "Boundary Value Analysis"? Explain with the help of an example. 10

5. (a) Draw the first 3 levels of DFDs for a "Student Information System". Make necessary assumptions. 10

(b) Write a short note on Software Re-engineering. 10

Master Of Computer Applications (MCA)
Chapter 4: Term-End Examination, June, 2023
MCS-213: Software Engineering

Time: 3 Hours
Maximum Marks: 100
Weightage: 70
Note: (i) Question No. 1 is compulsory.
(ii) Answer any three Questions from the rest.

1. (a) Explain the following approaches for the development of mobile applications: 10
(i) Native Application Development
(ii) Rapid Mobile Application Development (RMAD)
(iii) Progressive Web Applications (PWAs)
Also, mention any two advantages for each.

(b) Discuss the
(i) requirements related optimization and
(ii) architecture and design related optimizations in context of First Time Right (FTR) framework. 10

(c) In context to software project estimation, explain the following (highlighting their main tasks): 10
(i) Estimating the project-size
(ii) Estimating efforts
(iii) Estimating the schedule
(iv) Estimating the total cost

(d) Discuss the following software engineering models: 10
(i) Waterfall model
(ii) Spiral model

2. (a) Discuss the Human Computer Interface (HCI) and User Experience (UX) and designing for mobility aspects of software design phase. 10

(b) Explain defect metrics and maintainability metrics for measurement of software quality. 10

3. (a) Define cleanroom software engineering. List and explain the principles for the cleanroom-based software development. 10

(b) Explain the following emerging trends in software engineering highlighting their salient features, tools, technologies, purpose of usage and advantages: 10
(i) Low Code and No Code platforms
(ii) Containerization

4. (a) List and discuss the issues and challenges in management of web-based projects. 10

(b) Define CASE tools. What are the various categories of CASE tools available? Also mention the factors that affect their deployment in an organisation. 10

5. Write short notes on the following: 4×5=20
(a) Cloud platforms
(b) Continuous Delivery Model
(c) COCOMO Model
(d) Control Flow Graph (CFG) along with an example graph for any programming construct.

Master Of Computer Applications (MCA)
Chapter 5: Term-End Examination, December, 2023
MCS-213: Software Engineering

Time: 3 Hours
Maximum Marks: 100
Weightage: 70

Note: (i) Question No. 1 is compulsory.
(ii) Answer any three Questions from the rest.

1. (a) Describe the architectural design and modular design aspects of software design along with suitable diagrams. 10

(b) With the help of an example for each, explain the following Behavioural UML diagrams : 10
(i) Activity diagram
(ii) Use-case diagram

(c) Describe all the phases involved in data science life cycle. 10

(d) Define the re-engineering process. Narrate the process of re-engineering along with a block diagram and an example of use-case diagram. 10

2. (a) Define requirements engineering. What are the various tasks and processes involved in it ? Discuss functional and non-functional requirements in context to requirements engineering. 10

(b) Define software quality. List and elucidate some of the attributes of software quality. 10

3. (a) With reference to change control, briefly discuss the following : 10
(i) Change Management Process
(ii) Change Request
(iii) Change Control Report
(iv) Change Control Authority
(v) Engineering Change Order

(b) Define risk management. With reference to risk management, discuss risk manager tool, risk avoidance, risk detection and risk control. 10

4. (a) Discuss the project management related optimizations and development related optimization of First Time Right (FTR) framework. 10

(b) What are the basic drivers for innovations in software engineering ? Also list and discuss any *two* emerging trends in software engineering. 10

5. Write short notes on the following : 4×5=20
(a) Conversational Interfaces
(b) Rapid Mobile Application Development
(c) Prototype Model
(d) Putnam's model for estimation

Chapter 6: Most Asked Questions Part-A

1. What is software engineering, and why is it important in modern application development?
Answer: Software engineering is the application of systematic, disciplined, and quantifiable approaches to the development, operation, and maintenance of software. It ensures that complex software systems are reliable, efficient, and meet customer requirements. In today's world, where software powers critical systems from healthcare to banking, software engineering principles like modularity, scalability, and maintainability are crucial. MCA graduates must understand its importance in delivering high-quality, cost-effective software that can adapt to changing business and technological needs.

2. Explain the software development life cycle (SDLC) and its major phases.
Answer: The SDLC is a structured approach to software development that includes phases like requirement analysis, design, implementation, testing, deployment, and maintenance. Each phase serves a critical role in ensuring software meets user needs and performs reliably. MCA graduates should understand models like Waterfall, Agile, and Spiral to choose appropriate approaches for projects, balancing time, cost, and quality while adhering to industry standards and practices.

3. Discuss the differences between functional and non-functional requirements in software engineering.
Answer: Functional requirements define what a system should do, such as user authentication or payment processing, while non-functional requirements specify how the system performs tasks, covering aspects like performance, security, and usability. MCA graduates must document and prioritize both types effectively, as neglecting non-functional requirements can lead to software that meets functional goals but fails in real-world scenarios due to poor user experience or reliability.

4. What is software prototyping, and how does it benefit the development process?
Answer: Software prototyping involves creating an early version of a system to visualize and refine requirements. It helps stakeholders understand functionality and provide feedback before full-scale development. MCA graduates can leverage prototyping tools to reduce misunderstandings, minimize rework, and improve user satisfaction by involving end-users early in the process.

5. Explain the concept of software reusability and its advantages.
Answer: Software reusability means using existing software components to build new applications, reducing development time and costs. It promotes consistency and reliability as tested modules are reused. MCA graduates should design modular, well-documented code to enhance reusability, supporting efficient development in large-scale projects.

6. Discuss the significance of software metrics in measuring project quality and performance.
Answer: Software metrics are quantitative measures that assess software quality, productivity, and efficiency. Examples include lines of code (LOC), cyclomatic complexity, and defect density. MCA graduates must understand how to use these metrics to monitor progress, detect issues early, and ensure projects meet quality standards while staying within budget and timelines.

7. What is software maintenance, and why is it critical in the software lifecycle?
Answer: Software maintenance involves updating software post-deployment to fix bugs, improve performance, and adapt to new requirements or environments. It can consume up to 70% of the software lifecycle effort. MCA graduates should plan for maintainability during initial design, using modular architectures and thorough documentation to simplify future updates.

8. Explain the importance of risk management in software engineering projects.
Answer: Risk management identifies, analyzes, and mitigates potential issues that could derail software projects. Risks may include scope creep, technical failures, or resource shortages. MCA graduates must develop skills in risk assessment and mitigation strategies to ensure project success, delivering software on time and within budget despite uncertainties.

9. What is agile methodology, and how does it differ from traditional approaches?
Answer: Agile methodology emphasizes iterative development, customer collaboration, and adaptability to change. Unlike traditional Waterfall models, Agile breaks projects into smaller increments called sprints, enabling faster delivery and continuous feedback. MCA graduates must understand Agile principles to work effectively in dynamic environments and ensure software aligns with evolving user needs.

10. Discuss the ethical responsibilities of software engineers in developing secure systems.
Answer: Software engineers have a duty to protect user data and privacy, avoid intentional backdoors, and ensure systems resist cyberattacks. MCA graduates should follow ethical coding practices, adhere to data protection laws, and conduct thorough testing to build trust with users and safeguard organizational reputation.

11. Explain the role of CASE tools in software engineering.
Answer: Computer-Aided Software Engineering (CASE) tools automate various software development tasks such as design modeling, code generation, and testing. MCA graduates can use CASE tools to improve productivity, ensure consistency, and manage complex projects more efficiently.

12. What is the difference between verification and validation in software testing?
Answer: Verification ensures the product is built correctly (e.g., meeting design specifications), while validation checks if the right product is built (e.g., meeting user requirements). MCA graduates must understand both processes to deliver reliable software that aligns with user expectations and industry standards.

13. Discuss the advantages and challenges of using open-source software in projects.
Answer: Open-source software reduces costs and fosters innovation through community collaboration. However, it may pose risks like unclear licensing and lack of official support. MCA graduates must evaluate open-source tools carefully to balance benefits with potential challenges and ensure compliance with legal requirements.

14. Explain the concept of software configuration management (SCM).
Answer: SCM tracks and controls changes in software to maintain integrity throughout development. MCA graduates should use tools like Git for version control, enabling collaboration and preventing conflicts in multi-developer environments. SCM ensures consistency and facilitates debugging, rollback, and auditing.

15. What are software design patterns, and how do they benefit developers?
Answer: Design patterns are proven solutions to recurring software design problems. Examples include Singleton, Observer, and Factory patterns. MCA graduates should learn to apply these patterns to simplify complex designs, promote code reuse, and enhance system scalability and maintainability.

16. What is the difference between coupling and cohesion in software design?
Answer: Coupling refers to the degree of dependency between modules, while cohesion measures how closely related the functions within a module are. Low coupling and high cohesion are desirable as they lead to better modularity, easier maintenance, and greater flexibility. MCA graduates must strive for designs with minimal interdependencies between components while ensuring each module performs a well-defined task, which simplifies debugging and supports future enhancements.

17. Explain the waterfall model in software development and its advantages and limitations.
Answer: The waterfall model is a linear, sequential approach where each phase must be completed before the next begins. Advantages include clear documentation and structured processes, making it suitable for projects with well-defined requirements. However, its rigidity makes adapting to changes difficult. MCA graduates should use it in projects where requirements are stable and avoid it in dynamic environments that demand flexibility.

18. Discuss the importance of user interface (UI) design in software engineering.
Answer: UI design focuses on creating interfaces that are intuitive, efficient, and pleasant for users. A well-designed UI enhances usability, reduces errors, and improves user satisfaction. MCA graduates should learn human-computer interaction principles and design accessible, responsive interfaces to ensure the software is effective for diverse users and devices.

19. What is software quality assurance (SQA), and why is it critical?

Answer: SQA involves systematic activities to ensure software meets defined quality standards and user expectations. It includes process monitoring, code reviews, and testing strategies. MCA graduates should understand SQA to minimize defects, reduce development costs, and deliver reliable, high-performance software.

20. Explain the spiral model and how it manages risks in software development.
Answer: The spiral model combines iterative development with risk assessment at each phase. It allows continuous refinement of requirements and design based on feedback. MCA graduates should consider the spiral model for large, high-risk projects where early identification and mitigation of risks are essential to success.

21. Discuss software design principles that promote scalability and maintainability.
Answer: Principles like modularity, abstraction, encapsulation, and separation of concerns enhance scalability and maintainability. MCA graduates should apply these to design systems that can evolve with changing requirements and remain robust as they grow in size and complexity.

22. What is the role of feasibility studies in software project planning?
Answer: A feasibility study evaluates technical, economic, legal, operational, and scheduling aspects of a project. MCA graduates should conduct feasibility studies to determine whether a proposed system is viable and worth pursuing, helping stakeholders make informed decisions and avoid wasted resources.

23. Explain the significance of software documentation during the development lifecycle.
Answer: Documentation provides clear instructions, specifications, and insights about software functionality. It supports maintenance, knowledge transfer, and user onboarding. MCA graduates must create comprehensive documentation to facilitate collaboration and ensure the software remains understandable and maintainable over time.

24. What is the difference between black-box and white-box testing?
Answer: Black-box testing evaluates software functionality without knowing its internal structure, while white-box testing examines the internal code and logic. MCA graduates should use both approaches to detect a wide range of errors and ensure thorough validation of systems from multiple perspectives.

25. Discuss the ethical considerations software engineers should follow in their professional practice.
Answer: Ethical software engineers prioritize user safety, privacy, and fairness. MCA graduates should adhere to professional codes of conduct, avoid plagiarism, respect intellectual property, and ensure their work does not harm individuals or society. These practices build trust and contribute to a responsible software development culture.

26. Explain the concept of modular design and its benefits in software development.
Answer: Modular design involves breaking down software into independent, self-contained units that can be developed and tested separately. Benefits include easier debugging, improved code reuse, and faster development. MCA graduates should apply modularity to simplify complex projects and facilitate collaboration among team members.

27. What are the characteristics of good software?
Answer: Good software is reliable, efficient, secure, maintainable, and user-friendly. It meets functional requirements, performs optimally under varying conditions, and is adaptable to future needs. MCA graduates should focus on these characteristics to create high-quality software that delivers long-term value to users and stakeholders.

28. Discuss the advantages and disadvantages of agile software development.
Answer: Agile development promotes flexibility, continuous user feedback, and faster delivery of functional software. It supports collaboration and adapts well to changing requirements. However, it may lack formal documentation and can be challenging for large, distributed teams. MCA graduates should understand when Agile is appropriate and how to balance its strengths with potential challenges.

29. Explain software testing levels and their purposes.
Answer: Testing levels include unit testing (validates individual components), integration testing (checks interactions between modules), system testing (evaluates the entire system), and acceptance testing (ensures the system meets user requirements). MCA graduates should plan for all levels to detect defects early and ensure robust, reliable software delivery.

30. What is the role of software architects in large-scale projects?
Answer: Software architects design high-level system structures, define technology stacks, and ensure alignment with business goals. They make critical decisions that affect scalability, performance, and maintainability. MCA graduates aspiring to this role must develop skills in design patterns, system integration, and stakeholder communication to guide teams effectively.

31. What is software reliability, and how can it be achieved?
Answer: Software reliability refers to the probability of a system performing without failure under specified conditions for a defined period. It is achieved through rigorous testing, proper error handling, redundancy, and adherence to coding standards. MCA graduates must understand techniques like fault tolerance, reliability metrics, and preventive maintenance to ensure systems meet reliability requirements, especially in critical applications like healthcare and aviation.

32. Discuss the concept of version control systems (VCS) and their importance in software development.
Answer: Version control systems like Git track changes to code, enabling collaboration among developers and maintaining project history. They allow rollback to earlier versions, facilitate teamwork, and prevent conflicts in multi-developer environments. MCA graduates must master VCS to ensure efficient workflow management, especially in large and distributed teams working on complex projects.

33. Explain the difference between adaptive and corrective software maintenance.
Answer: Adaptive maintenance involves modifying software to remain compatible with changing environments, such as operating system updates. Corrective maintenance fixes bugs or errors detected in the software after deployment. MCA graduates should plan for both in their projects to ensure long-term system performance and user satisfaction.

34. What is software reuse, and how does it improve productivity?
Answer: Software reuse involves utilizing existing software components, frameworks, or libraries to build new systems. It reduces development time, improves reliability, and cuts costs since reused components are often well-tested. MCA graduates should learn to design reusable modules and integrate them effectively to enhance productivity in software projects.

35. Discuss the differences between structured and object-oriented software design.
Answer: Structured design emphasizes process-oriented decomposition, while object-oriented design organizes systems around data and behavior encapsulated in objects. MCA graduates should understand the strengths of object-oriented design, such as modularity and reusability, making it the preferred approach for modern, large-scale applications.

36. Explain the concept of risk analysis in software project management.
Answer: Risk analysis identifies potential problems that could impact project success, such as technical challenges, resource constraints, or market changes. MCA graduates must learn to assess the probability and impact of risks, prioritize them, and develop mitigation plans to minimize disruptions and ensure smooth project delivery.

37. What are software project estimation techniques, and why are they important?
Answer: Estimation techniques like Function Point Analysis (FPA), COCOMO, and expert judgment predict effort, time, and cost for software projects. MCA graduates should master these methods to provide accurate estimates, enabling better planning, budgeting, and resource allocation, which are critical for successful project management.

38. Discuss the importance of software process models in guiding development activities.
Answer: Process models like Waterfall, Agile, Spiral, and RAD provide structured approaches to software development, ensuring consistency, quality, and predictability. MCA graduates should understand when to apply each model based on project size, complexity, and stakeholder requirements to achieve optimal results.

39. What is software scalability, and how can it be designed into systems?
Answer: Scalability is the ability of software to handle increasing workloads without performance degradation. MCA graduates should design systems with modular architectures, load balancing, and database optimization to ensure applications can grow seamlessly with user demands and business needs.

40. Explain the role of software testing tools in ensuring quality.
Answer: Software testing tools like Selenium, JUnit, and LoadRunner automate test cases, improve accuracy, and reduce manual effort. MCA graduates should learn to use these tools for various testing stages—unit, integration, performance—to deliver high-quality software efficiently and consistently.

41. Discuss how software requirement specification (SRS) documents aid development.
Answer: An SRS document defines functional and non-functional requirements, serving as a blueprint for developers and testers. MCA graduates should know how to prepare clear, comprehensive SRS documents to avoid misunderstandings, reduce scope creep, and ensure software aligns with stakeholder expectations.

42. What is software validation, and how does it differ from verification?
Answer: Validation ensures the software meets user needs and intended use, while verification checks if it conforms to design specifications. MCA graduates must apply both to deliver software that is correct, functional, and satisfactory to end-users, preventing costly errors post-deployment.

43. Explain the concept of software portability and its significance.
Answer: Software portability refers to the ease with which software can run on different platforms or environments without significant modification. MCA graduates should design platform-independent systems using standard technologies and coding practices to ensure wider usability and reduced redevelopment costs.

44. What are software project milestones, and why are they essential?
Answer: Milestones are significant checkpoints in a project that signify progress, such as completing design or testing phases. MCA graduates must use milestones to track progress, identify delays early, and keep stakeholders informed, ensuring timely and efficient project completion.

45. Discuss the ethical considerations of using open-source libraries in proprietary software.
Answer: While open-source libraries accelerate development, using them in proprietary software requires adherence to licensing terms. MCA graduates must ensure compliance with licenses like GPL or MIT to avoid legal issues and respect the rights of original contributors.

46. Explain the concept of software modularity and how it aids maintainability.
Answer: Modularity divides software into independent, cohesive units, simplifying development and maintenance. MCA graduates should design systems with clear module boundaries to enable easier debugging, testing, and updating, ensuring software remains manageable over time.

47. What are the key differences between software engineering and traditional engineering?
Answer: Software engineering deals with intangible, evolving products, whereas traditional engineering involves physical, static structures. MCA graduates must understand that software development requires iterative refinement, continuous user feedback, and adaptive processes to succeed in dynamic environments.

48. Discuss the significance of software audits in ensuring compliance and quality.
Answer: Software audits assess adherence to standards, policies, and legal requirements. MCA graduates should support audits to ensure systems are secure, maintainable, and compliant with industry regulations, minimizing organizational risks and building user trust.

49. Explain the importance of scalability testing in modern software applications.
Answer: Scalability testing assesses how software performs under increasing loads. MCA graduates must conduct such tests to identify bottlenecks and optimize systems for growth, especially for cloud-based and high-traffic applications where performance under stress is critical.

50. What is software re-engineering, and when is it necessary?
Answer: Software re-engineering involves modifying existing software to improve performance, maintainability, or adapt to new environments. MCA graduates should recommend re-engineering for legacy systems that are critical to business but built on outdated technologies.

51. What is software process improvement, and why is it essential?
Answer: Software process improvement involves enhancing development processes to increase efficiency, quality, and customer satisfaction. Frameworks like CMMI (Capability Maturity Model Integration) guide organizations in assessing and refining their practices. MCA graduates must understand these concepts to help organizations minimize defects, reduce development costs, and remain competitive in dynamic markets.

52. Explain the concept of software reverse engineering and its applications.
Answer: Reverse engineering involves analyzing software to understand its design and functionality, often for maintenance, security analysis, or interoperability. MCA graduates should understand its ethical and legal boundaries, ensuring such techniques are used responsibly, such as recovering legacy code without violating intellectual property rights.

53. Discuss the importance of user acceptance testing (UAT) in software deployment.
Answer: UAT ensures software meets user requirements and functions correctly in real-world scenarios before deployment. MCA graduates must work with stakeholders during UAT to gather feedback, identify overlooked issues, and ensure the system delivers value and user satisfaction.

54. What is the difference between iterative and incremental software development models?
Answer: Iterative models focus on refining software through repeated cycles, while incremental models deliver functional parts of the system in stages. MCA graduates should combine both approaches where appropriate to achieve faster delivery and continuous improvement in projects.

55. Explain how software configuration management (SCM) supports team collaboration.
Answer: SCM tools like Git enable developers to track changes, manage code versions, and collaborate efficiently without conflicts. MCA graduates must master SCM practices to ensure consistency, traceability, and smooth teamwork in modern distributed development environments.

56. Discuss the benefits and challenges of outsourcing in software development.
Answer: Outsourcing can reduce costs and provide access to specialized skills but may lead to communication issues and reduced control. MCA graduates should learn strategies to manage outsourced projects effectively, such as clear documentation, regular reviews, and secure data sharing.

57. What is the significance of the ISO 9001 standard in software engineering?
Answer: ISO 9001 sets quality management standards that help organizations improve processes and customer satisfaction. MCA graduates should understand its principles to design and implement quality-focused practices in software projects, ensuring compliance and global recognition.

58. Explain the concept of design validation and verification in software engineering.
Answer: Validation checks if the software meets user needs, while verification ensures compliance with design specifications. MCA graduates must conduct both processes to prevent costly errors and ensure high-quality, user-centric solutions.

59. What is the role of software architects in ensuring system scalability?
Answer: Software architects design system structures to support growth without performance degradation. MCA graduates aspiring to this role must develop skills in distributed systems, database optimization, and load balancing to build scalable applications for high-demand environments.

60. Discuss the ethical challenges of developing software for surveillance purposes.
Answer: Surveillance software may infringe on privacy rights if misused. MCA graduates must balance legal compliance and ethical responsibilities, ensuring transparency, secure data handling, and avoiding systems that facilitate mass surveillance without due process.

61. What are software performance metrics, and how are they used?
Answer: Performance metrics measure system attributes like response time, throughput, and resource utilization. MCA graduates should monitor these metrics to identify bottlenecks, optimize applications, and ensure systems meet user expectations for speed and reliability.

62. Explain how CASE tools assist in software development lifecycle management.
Answer: CASE tools automate tasks like requirement analysis, design modeling, and testing, increasing efficiency and accuracy. MCA graduates should leverage these tools to handle complex projects, maintain consistency, and reduce manual errors in software engineering workflows.

63. Discuss the importance of software scalability testing for enterprise applications.
Answer: Scalability testing ensures software can handle increasing loads, user traffic, and data volumes. MCA graduates should conduct such tests early to design systems that grow with organizational needs, avoiding performance degradation and system failures under stress.

64. What is software usability engineering, and why is it important?
Answer: Usability engineering focuses on designing software that is intuitive and user-friendly. MCA graduates must incorporate user feedback, accessibility standards, and interface testing to build systems that enhance user experience and reduce learning curves.

65. Explain the difference between structured walkthroughs and code inspections.
Answer: Structured walkthroughs involve reviewing designs or documents with team members for feedback, while code inspections focus on detecting errors in source code. MCA graduates should employ both techniques to improve quality and reduce defects before deployment.

66. Discuss the role of software prototypes in managing customer expectations.
Answer: Prototypes provide early visualizations of system features, helping stakeholders clarify requirements and provide feedback. MCA graduates should use prototypes to align development with customer expectations and avoid costly changes later in the process.

67. What are the advantages of component-based software engineering (CBSE)?
Answer: CBSE promotes reuse of pre-built components, accelerating development and enhancing reliability. MCA graduates must learn how to integrate components effectively, addressing challenges like compatibility and customization for specific project needs.

68. Explain the concept of software fault tolerance and its significance.
Answer: Fault tolerance allows systems to continue operating despite hardware or software failures. MCA graduates should design systems with redundancy, failover mechanisms, and error recovery processes to ensure reliability in critical applications.

69. Discuss the significance of software audit trails in secure applications.
Answer: Audit trails record user activities and system events, supporting security, compliance, and troubleshooting. MCA graduates should implement robust logging mechanisms to detect unauthorized actions and support forensic analysis in case of breaches.

70. What is the role of UML diagrams in software design?
Answer: UML diagrams visualize system architecture, behavior, and interactions, aiding communication among stakeholders. MCA graduates should master UML tools to design complex systems clearly and facilitate effective team collaboration.

71. Explain the purpose of regression testing in software maintenance.
Answer: Regression testing ensures new changes don't break existing functionality. MCA graduates should automate regression tests to quickly verify system stability after updates or bug fixes, reducing deployment risks.

72. Discuss the advantages of pair programming in Agile software development.
Answer: Pair programming improves code quality, facilitates knowledge sharing, and reduces defects. MCA graduates should embrace this practice to enhance collaboration and gain peer insights in fast-paced Agile environments.

73. What is software portability testing, and when is it required?

Answer: Portability testing verifies if software functions correctly across different platforms and environments. MCA graduates should conduct such tests for applications intended for multiple operating systems or devices to ensure broad usability.

74. Explain the concept of software reliability growth models.
Answer: Reliability growth models predict defect trends and improvement over time as issues are fixed. MCA graduates should use these models during testing phases to assess system stability and plan release schedules effectively.

75. Discuss the ethical responsibilities of software engineers in preventing software piracy.
Answer: Software engineers must implement licensing mechanisms, encryption, and anti-tampering techniques to prevent piracy. MCA graduates should educate users on legal software use and advocate ethical practices that respect intellectual property rights.

76. What is software risk management, and how is it implemented?
Answer: Software risk management involves identifying, assessing, and mitigating potential issues that could impact project success. Steps include risk identification, analysis, prioritization, and developing mitigation plans. MCA graduates should implement risk registers, conduct regular reviews, and use tools like FMEA (Failure Mode and Effects Analysis) to proactively address uncertainties in projects and reduce potential negative impacts on timelines, budgets, and quality.

77. Discuss the significance of software modularization in large-scale systems.
Answer: Modularization divides software into independent, cohesive units that simplify development, testing, and maintenance. MCA graduates should apply modular design principles to enable parallel development, improve code reusability, and make large systems more manageable. Modularization also enhances scalability and reduces the impact of changes in complex projects.

78. Explain the concept of software fault injection and its role in testing.
Answer: Fault injection deliberately introduces errors into a system to evaluate its robustness and error-handling capabilities. MCA graduates should use this technique to identify vulnerabilities, test fault-tolerance mechanisms, and ensure systems can recover gracefully from unexpected failures. It's particularly valuable for critical systems like healthcare and aviation software.

79. What is software re-engineering, and how does it differ from reverse engineering?
Answer: Software re-engineering improves or restructures existing software to enhance maintainability and performance, while reverse engineering analyzes software to understand its design and functionality. MCA graduates should apply re-engineering for legacy systems that need modernization and ensure compliance with intellectual property laws when performing reverse engineering.

80. Discuss the advantages and limitations of the V-model in software development.
Answer: The V-model emphasizes verification and validation at each stage of development, ensuring defects are caught early. Its advantages include improved quality and clear phase relationships, but it lacks flexibility for evolving requirements. MCA graduates should apply the V-model in projects with stable specifications but prefer Agile for dynamic environments.

81. Explain the significance of software security testing in modern applications.
Answer: Security testing identifies vulnerabilities that could lead to unauthorized access, data breaches, or system compromise. MCA graduates must conduct penetration testing, static code analysis, and threat modeling to safeguard applications, especially in domains handling sensitive data like finance or healthcare.

82. What is software benchmarking, and why is it important?
Answer: Benchmarking compares software performance against predefined standards or competitors to identify areas for improvement. MCA graduates should use benchmarking to assess speed, efficiency, and scalability, ensuring their systems meet or exceed industry standards.

83. Discuss the role of software development standards like IEEE in ensuring quality.

Answer: Standards like IEEE 830 (SRS) and IEEE 1016 (design documentation) provide guidelines for consistency, clarity, and quality in software development. MCA graduates should follow these standards to align projects with industry best practices and ensure reliable, maintainable systems.

84. Explain the concept of software reuse libraries and their benefits.
Answer: Software reuse libraries store pre-built components that developers can integrate into projects. MCA graduates should learn to leverage these libraries to accelerate development, reduce errors, and promote consistency across applications, especially in enterprise environments.

85. What is software portability, and how can developers ensure it?
Answer: Portability is the ease with which software can operate on various platforms with minimal modifications. MCA graduates can achieve this by using platform-independent languages, avoiding proprietary APIs, and conducting thorough portability testing during development.

86. Discuss the importance of code refactoring in maintaining software quality.
Answer: Refactoring improves code structure without altering its functionality, making it cleaner, more efficient, and easier to maintain. MCA graduates should practice regular refactoring to prevent technical debt, enhance readability, and support long-term scalability of software systems.

87. Explain how software evolution impacts the development lifecycle.
Answer: Software evolves to adapt to changing requirements, technologies, and user needs. MCA graduates must design systems with flexibility and maintainability in mind, enabling smooth updates and minimizing disruption during evolution phases.

88. What are the key characteristics of agile software development teams?
Answer: Agile teams are cross-functional, collaborative, and adaptive to change. MCA graduates should embrace Agile values like customer collaboration, iterative delivery, and continuous improvement to thrive in dynamic development environments and deliver user-centric solutions.

89. Discuss the significance of software project monitoring and control in project management.
Answer: Monitoring and control ensure projects stay on schedule, within budget, and aligned with objectives. MCA graduates should use metrics, dashboards, and tools like Earned Value Analysis (EVA) to track progress and make informed decisions to mitigate deviations effectively.

90. Explain the concept of software defect density and its relevance.
Answer: Defect density measures the number of defects per unit size of software, such as lines of code. MCA graduates should monitor this metric to assess software quality and identify modules needing more rigorous testing or redesign.

91. What is software concurrency, and why is it important?
Answer: Concurrency enables multiple processes to execute simultaneously, improving performance in multi-core systems. MCA graduates should understand concurrency principles and synchronization techniques to design responsive, scalable applications, especially for real-time and distributed systems.

92. Discuss the role of software frameworks in accelerating application development.
Answer: Frameworks provide reusable structures and components that simplify development tasks. MCA graduates should learn to use frameworks like Spring for Java or Django for Python to accelerate workflows, maintain consistency, and reduce boilerplate code.

93. Explain how software engineers can ensure accessibility compliance in their applications.
Answer: Accessibility compliance ensures software is usable by people with disabilities. MCA graduates should apply standards like WCAG (Web Content Accessibility Guidelines), design intuitive interfaces, and test with assistive technologies to create inclusive systems.

94. What is the significance of software process automation in modern engineering?

Answer: Process automation reduces manual effort, increases efficiency, and minimizes human errors. MCA graduates should leverage tools like CI/CD pipelines to automate testing, builds, and deployments for faster, reliable software delivery.

95. Discuss the ethical considerations in software project bidding and estimation.
Answer: Software engineers must provide honest estimates, avoiding underquoting or overpromising. MCA graduates should follow ethical practices by assessing risks realistically and ensuring transparency in cost and time projections to build trust with stakeholders.

96. Explain how software scalability challenges differ in monolithic and microservices architectures.
Answer: Monolithic systems scale by replicating the entire application, which can be inefficient. Microservices allow scaling individual components independently. MCA graduates should analyze trade-offs to choose architectures that align with scalability needs and resource constraints.

97. What is software middleware, and how does it support application integration?
Answer: Middleware acts as a bridge between different applications, enabling communication and data exchange. MCA graduates should learn to use middleware like message brokers and API gateways to integrate heterogeneous systems in enterprise environments.

98. Discuss the role of design thinking in modern software engineering.
Answer: Design thinking emphasizes empathy, ideation, and prototyping to solve user problems innovatively. MCA graduates should apply this approach to build user-centered software that aligns with real-world needs and encourages creativity in development.

99. Explain how DevOps practices influence software quality and delivery.
Answer: DevOps integrates development and operations to streamline workflows, enabling faster, more reliable software releases. MCA graduates should adopt DevOps tools and practices like continuous integration and automated testing to enhance collaboration and software quality.

100. What is software documentation debt, and how can it be avoided?
Answer: Documentation debt occurs when inadequate or outdated documentation hinders understanding and maintenance. MCA graduates should document code and processes consistently, using tools like wikis and automated documentation generators to avoid this common issue.

101. What is software project scope, and why is scope management important?
Answer: Software project scope defines the boundaries, deliverables, and objectives of a project. Effective scope management ensures projects stay aligned with stakeholder expectations, prevents scope creep, and manages resources efficiently. MCA graduates must master scope management techniques, including clear documentation and change control processes, to deliver projects on time and within budget while meeting quality standards.

102. Explain the concept of technical debt and its impact on software development.
Answer: Technical debt arises when developers choose shortcuts or quick fixes that compromise long-term software quality. While it accelerates delivery initially, it leads to increased maintenance costs and system instability over time. MCA graduates must understand how to balance speed and quality, adopting practices like refactoring and code reviews to minimize technical debt in projects.

103. Discuss the differences between software product and software project.
Answer: A software product is designed for a broad audience and sold as a package, while a software project is developed for a specific client's needs. MCA graduates should understand these distinctions to tailor development processes, as products demand scalability and general usability, whereas projects focus on customized solutions.

104. What is software system integration testing, and why is it critical?
Answer: System integration testing ensures that different modules or subsystems work together correctly as a whole. It identifies interface issues, data flow errors, and communication mismatches. MCA graduates must plan and execute integration tests carefully to ensure seamless system operation and prevent failures in production environments.

105. Explain the role of middleware in distributed software systems.
Answer: Middleware facilitates communication and data exchange between different components in distributed systems. It provides services like authentication, messaging, and API management. MCA graduates should understand middleware's importance in enabling interoperability, scalability, and simplified development of complex distributed applications.

106. Discuss the importance of software cost-benefit analysis in project planning.
Answer: Cost-benefit analysis evaluates whether a software project's expected benefits justify its costs. MCA graduates should conduct such analyses to help stakeholders make informed decisions, prioritize investments, and ensure resource allocation aligns with business goals.

107. What is continuous integration (CI), and how does it improve software quality?
Answer: CI is a DevOps practice where developers integrate code changes frequently into a shared repository, triggering automated builds and tests. MCA graduates must adopt CI to detect errors early, improve collaboration, and deliver more reliable software faster.

108. Explain the concept of software design consistency and its significance.
Answer: Design consistency ensures uniformity in software interfaces, structures, and behavior. It enhances usability, simplifies maintenance, and prevents errors. MCA graduates should establish design standards and enforce them through style guides and code reviews for high-quality software delivery.

109. What are the advantages and disadvantages of Rapid Application Development (RAD)?
Answer: RAD enables faster software delivery through prototyping and iterative development. It suits projects with dynamic requirements but may sacrifice scalability and thorough documentation. MCA graduates should use RAD for small, time-sensitive projects but carefully assess its fit for complex systems.

110. Discuss the ethical responsibilities of software engineers in managing user data privacy.
Answer: Software engineers must protect user data against unauthorized access and misuse. MCA graduates should adhere to privacy laws like GDPR, implement encryption, and design systems that allow users control over their data to maintain ethical standards and build trust.

111. What is software localization, and why is it important?
Answer: Localization adapts software for different languages, regions, and cultures to enhance user experience globally. MCA graduates must design systems with localization support to cater to diverse user bases, ensuring software's accessibility and acceptance in multiple markets.

112. Explain the concept of defect tracking systems and their role in quality assurance.
Answer: Defect tracking systems like JIRA record, prioritize, and monitor software bugs throughout the development lifecycle. MCA graduates should use these tools to streamline bug resolution, improve communication among teams, and maintain high-quality software standards.

113. Discuss the impact of cloud computing on software engineering practices.
Answer: Cloud computing changes how software is developed, deployed, and maintained, enabling scalability, on-demand resources, and continuous delivery. MCA graduates must learn cloud-native architectures and practices to design systems optimized for modern cloud environments.

114. What is the significance of software architecture patterns in large-scale systems?
Answer: Architecture patterns like MVC, Microservices, and Layered Architecture provide proven structures for building scalable and maintainable systems. MCA graduates should understand these patterns to design robust solutions for complex, enterprise-level applications.

115. Explain the differences between software validation and user acceptance testing (UAT).
Answer: Validation ensures software meets its intended purpose, while UAT verifies that it satisfies user requirements and is ready for deployment. MCA graduates must collaborate with end-users during UAT to ensure systems are practical, functional, and user-friendly.

116. Discuss the benefits and limitations of using open-source software in enterprise systems.
Answer: Open-source software reduces costs and fosters innovation but may lack official support and consistent updates. MCA graduates should evaluate open-source components carefully for security, license compatibility, and suitability before integrating them into enterprise systems.

117. What is software scalability testing, and how is it conducted?
Answer: Scalability testing assesses software's ability to handle growth in users, data, and transactions without performance degradation. MCA graduates should simulate increasing loads using tools like JMeter and identify potential bottlenecks for optimization.

118. Explain the importance of using API design best practices in modern software systems.
Answer: APIs connect systems and enable seamless integration. MCA graduates should apply best practices like RESTful design, versioning, and security measures to build robust, scalable, and developer-friendly APIs that foster interoperability and innovation.

119. Discuss the role of ethical hacking in improving software security.
Answer: Ethical hacking identifies vulnerabilities before malicious actors exploit them. MCA graduates should engage in ethical hacking within legal frameworks to strengthen systems, implement countermeasures, and ensure compliance with cybersecurity standards.

120. What are software acceptance criteria, and why are they crucial?
Answer: Acceptance criteria define conditions a software product must meet to be considered complete. MCA graduates should collaborate with stakeholders to establish clear, measurable criteria to avoid misunderstandings and ensure successful project delivery.

121. Explain the concept of software concurrency and its challenges.
Answer: Concurrency enables simultaneous execution of multiple processes, improving performance but introducing challenges like race conditions and deadlocks. MCA graduates must design systems with proper synchronization techniques to ensure correctness and efficiency.

122. What is the significance of documentation in Agile software development?
Answer: Agile emphasizes working software over extensive documentation but still requires essential records like user stories and API references. MCA graduates should maintain lightweight, up-to-date documentation to support collaboration and future maintenance.

123. Discuss how software engineers can design systems for high availability (HA).
Answer: High availability ensures systems remain operational despite failures. MCA graduates should design HA systems using redundancy, load balancing, and failover mechanisms to minimize downtime and maintain user trust in critical applications.

124. What are the benefits of code reviews in software development teams?
Answer: Code reviews improve quality, promote knowledge sharing, and reduce defects. MCA graduates should participate in peer reviews to learn best practices, catch issues early, and foster a collaborative development culture.

125. Explain the differences between monolithic and microservices architectures in software design.
Answer: Monolithic architectures combine all functions in a single codebase, while microservices divide applications into independent services. MCA graduates should choose architectures based on project needs, considering scalability, maintainability, and deployment flexibility.

126. Analyze how software engineers can design robust systems to handle hardware failures gracefully.
Answer: Hardware failures can disrupt software operations, causing downtime or data loss. MCA graduates should design systems with redundancy, such as RAID for storage and failover servers for critical applications. Incorporating error detection and recovery mechanisms like checkpointing helps ensure minimal disruption. Regular stress testing and monitoring tools can predict hardware issues, allowing proactive mitigation strategies.

127. Discuss the ethical implications of predictive analytics in employee monitoring software.

Answer: Predictive analytics can improve productivity but may invade privacy and create distrust. MCA graduates must design systems that anonymize data, respect employee consent, and comply with labor laws. Transparency in data collection and ethical usage policies ensure monitoring tools are balanced and not overly intrusive.

128. Explain how to ensure consistency in distributed database systems.
Answer: Distributed databases face challenges in maintaining data consistency across nodes. MCA graduates should implement techniques like eventual consistency, quorum-based replication, or consensus algorithms (e.g., Paxos, Raft). Careful trade-offs between consistency, availability, and partition tolerance (CAP theorem) are essential for robust systems.

129. Discuss how software engineers can ethically handle user feedback containing sensitive personal information.
Answer: User feedback may unintentionally include private data. MCA graduates should filter and anonymize feedback, implement secure storage, and limit access to authorized personnel only. Ethical practices include informing users about data handling policies and adhering to data protection regulations.

130. Analyze the role of containerization in improving software deployment workflows.
Answer: Containers like Docker provide isolated environments for running applications, ensuring consistency across development and production. MCA graduates should use container orchestration tools like Kubernetes for scaling and automating deployments. Containers enhance portability and reduce dependency issues, making deployment workflows faster and more reliable.

131. Explain how software engineers can design energy-efficient algorithms for wearable devices.
Answer: Wearable devices have limited battery life and processing power. MCA graduates should design algorithms that minimize CPU usage, reduce network communication, and leverage low-power hardware states. Techniques like duty cycling and edge processing improve energy efficiency while maintaining functionality.

132. Discuss how to mitigate ethical concerns in recommendation systems for streaming platforms.
Answer: Recommendation systems can create filter bubbles or promote addictive content. MCA graduates should design systems that offer diverse content, allow user control over recommendations, and prioritize transparency in algorithmic decisions to promote ethical engagement.

133. Explain how software engineers can address the challenge of data synchronization in offline-first applications.
Answer: Offline-first applications must synchronize data between local storage and servers when connectivity resumes. MCA graduates should use conflict resolution strategies, timestamp-based synchronization, and robust error-handling to ensure data integrity during sync processes.

134. Discuss the importance of usability testing in enterprise software development.
Answer: Usability testing ensures software aligns with user workflows and minimizes errors. MCA graduates should involve actual users in testing, collect feedback on navigation and accessibility, and iterate designs to improve user satisfaction and productivity in enterprise systems.

135. Analyze how software engineers can implement zero-trust security models in enterprise applications.
Answer: Zero-trust security assumes no implicit trust within a network. MCA graduates should enforce strict authentication, use micro-segmentation, and monitor all activities to secure systems against internal and external threats effectively.

136. Discuss ethical considerations in developing deepfake detection software.
Answer: While deepfake detection combats misinformation, it must avoid misuse, such as censorship or privacy violations. MCA graduates should ensure ethical deployment, educate users about limitations, and advocate for transparency in combating harmful content.

137. Explain how to manage concurrency issues in multi-threaded applications.

Answer: Concurrency issues like race conditions and deadlocks occur when threads access shared resources improperly. MCA graduates should use synchronization primitives like mutexes, semaphores, and thread-safe data structures to manage concurrency safely.

138. Analyze how software engineers can support digital literacy in rural areas using mobile apps.
Answer: Mobile apps for rural users should have intuitive interfaces, support local languages, and work offline. MCA graduates should design lightweight apps optimized for low-bandwidth networks and include educational content to promote digital literacy effectively.

139. Discuss the role of edge computing in enhancing IoT systems.
Answer: Edge computing processes data near the source, reducing latency and bandwidth use. MCA graduates should design IoT systems leveraging edge devices to ensure faster responses and scalability, especially in time-critical applications like autonomous vehicles.

140. Explain how software engineers can secure blockchain-based applications.
Answer: Blockchain offers inherent security but is vulnerable at integration points. MCA graduates should secure smart contracts through audits, protect private keys with hardware wallets, and design consensus mechanisms resistant to attacks like 51% attacks.

141. Discuss how ethical frameworks guide software engineers in designing AI for medical diagnosis.
Answer: AI in healthcare requires transparency, accuracy, and accountability. MCA graduates should ensure data privacy, avoid biases in training datasets, and involve medical professionals to validate AI recommendations ethically.

142. Analyze how to design fault-isolated microservices architectures.
Answer: Fault isolation ensures failures in one service don't cascade to others. MCA graduates should implement circuit breakers, service meshes, and redundancy in microservices to improve resilience and system stability.

143. Explain how software engineers can support green computing initiatives in data centers.
Answer: Green computing reduces environmental impact. MCA graduates should optimize software for energy efficiency, use load balancing to prevent server overuse, and design algorithms that minimize computational overhead in data centers.

144. Discuss the challenges of developing real-time collaboration tools like online editors.
Answer: Real-time collaboration tools require low latency, conflict resolution, and secure communication. MCA graduates should implement operational transformation (OT) or conflict-free replicated data types (CRDTs) to ensure seamless multi-user editing.

145. Explain how software engineers can design systems to comply with anti-money laundering (AML) regulations.
Answer: AML compliance requires monitoring transactions for suspicious activities. MCA graduates should design systems with transaction limits, anomaly detection algorithms, and reporting tools to comply with financial regulations effectively.

146. Analyze the ethical implications of using biometric authentication in consumer devices.
Answer: Biometric data is sensitive and difficult to replace if compromised. MCA graduates should ensure secure storage using encryption, allow alternative authentication methods, and obtain explicit user consent to address privacy concerns.

147. Discuss how software engineers can design scalable chat applications for global users.
Answer: Global chat apps need real-time messaging, low latency, and horizontal scalability. MCA graduates should use WebSockets, distributed databases, and sharding techniques to support millions of concurrent users worldwide.

148. Explain how to secure APIs in healthcare systems handling sensitive patient data.
Answer: APIs in healthcare must comply with privacy regulations like HIPAA. MCA graduates should use token-based authentication, encrypt data in transit, and perform regular penetration testing to secure APIs effectively.

149. Discuss how software engineers can design user-centric interfaces for elderly users.
Answer: Elderly users benefit from simple, intuitive designs with larger text, high-contrast themes, and minimal clutter. MCA graduates should conduct usability testing with elderly participants to ensure accessibility and ease of use.

150. Analyze the role of ethical considerations in designing gamified learning platforms for children.
Answer: Gamification engages children but risks promoting addiction. MCA graduates should design platforms that balance fun with educational goals, avoid manipulative reward systems, and ensure parental controls for safe usage.

151. Explain how software engineers can address latency issues in AR/VR applications.
Answer: AR/VR apps require ultra-low latency to prevent motion sickness. MCA graduates should use optimized rendering pipelines, edge computing, and predictive algorithms to ensure seamless user experiences.

152. Discuss how software engineers can implement robust audit trails in financial software.
Answer: Audit trails track user actions for compliance and fraud detection. MCA graduates should design secure, immutable logs and ensure logs are encrypted and accessible only to authorized personnel.

153. Analyze the challenges of ensuring ethical AI behavior in autonomous drones.
Answer: Autonomous drones require ethical programming to handle unforeseen scenarios like collision avoidance. MCA graduates should implement decision-making frameworks prioritizing safety and align drone behavior with legal and ethical guidelines.

154. Explain how software engineers can design effective disaster recovery plans for cloud-based applications.
Answer: Disaster recovery involves backups, replication, and failover systems. MCA graduates should design multi-region deployments, automate recovery procedures, and test plans regularly to ensure readiness during outages.

155. Discuss how to balance software localization with cultural sensitivity.
Answer: Localization adapts software for different languages and regions but must avoid cultural misinterpretations. MCA graduates should involve native speakers and cultural experts to ensure translations and designs are contextually appropriate.

156. Explain how software engineers can prevent privilege escalation attacks in enterprise systems.
Answer: Privilege escalation allows attackers unauthorized access. MCA graduates should enforce least privilege principles, regularly audit user permissions, and use multi-factor authentication to minimize risks.

157. Discuss the ethical challenges in deploying AI chatbots for mental health support.
Answer: AI chatbots lack empathy and may fail in critical scenarios. MCA graduates should set clear limitations, involve human counselors for escalations, and prioritize user privacy to ensure ethical deployment in mental health services.

158. Analyze how software engineers can optimize database queries in high-transaction environments.
Answer: Optimizing queries reduces latency and resource consumption. MCA graduates should use indexing, caching, and query profiling tools to fine-tune database performance in high-load systems.

159. Explain how to design privacy-preserving data sharing systems using differential privacy.
Answer: Differential privacy adds noise to datasets, protecting individual identities. MCA graduates should integrate this technique in data-sharing systems to enable analytics without compromising user privacy.

160. Discuss the role of ethical design in developing persuasive fitness apps.
Answer: Persuasive fitness apps encourage healthy habits but must avoid overburdening users. MCA graduates should design positive reinforcement mechanisms and allow users to customize goals, respecting autonomy and mental well-being.

161. Analyze how software engineers can secure serverless applications from common vulnerabilities.
Answer: Serverless apps face risks like insecure configurations and event injection. MCA graduates should validate inputs, limit permissions, and monitor cloud provider logs to secure serverless environments.

162. Explain how to design scalable video conferencing solutions for remote teams.
Answer: Scalable video conferencing requires efficient codecs, adaptive bitrate streaming, and distributed servers. MCA graduates should use WebRTC and edge computing for real-time, high-quality communication.

163. Discuss ethical issues in collecting biometric data for workplace attendance systems.
Answer: Biometric attendance raises privacy concerns if data is misused. MCA graduates should ensure data is encrypted, limit retention periods, and provide alternative methods for employees uncomfortable with biometrics.

164. Explain how software engineers can balance innovation and ethical constraints in AR advertising.
Answer: AR ads enhance user engagement but may intrude on personal spaces. MCA graduates should design opt-in systems, clearly label advertisements, and avoid manipulative techniques to respect user autonomy.

165. Analyze how software engineers can support compliance with anti-spam regulations in email platforms.
Answer: Anti-spam laws like CAN-SPAM require explicit consent for marketing emails. MCA graduates should implement double opt-in systems, provide unsubscribe options, and monitor for spam reports to ensure compliance.

166. Discuss the challenges of debugging distributed systems.
Answer: Debugging distributed systems is complex due to asynchronous operations and multiple failure points. MCA graduates should use centralized logging, tracing tools, and simulation environments to troubleshoot effectively.

167. Explain how software engineers can design ethical persuasive elements in e-learning apps.
Answer: Persuasive design in e-learning motivates learners but must avoid addiction. MCA graduates should use ethical gamification techniques, focus on skill-building, and allow users control over their learning paths.

168. Discuss how to secure sensitive healthcare data in multi-tenant cloud applications.
Answer: Multi-tenant healthcare apps require strict data isolation and encryption. MCA graduates should use tenant-aware access controls and comply with healthcare regulations like HIPAA for secure operations.

169. Analyze how software engineers can support accessibility in AI-driven interfaces.
Answer: AI interfaces should support assistive technologies like screen readers and voice commands. MCA graduates should test with diverse users and follow accessibility standards (WCAG) for inclusive designs.

170. Explain how to implement end-to-end encryption in messaging applications.
Answer: End-to-end encryption ensures only intended recipients can read messages. MCA graduates should use protocols like Signal, securely manage encryption keys, and prevent metadata leaks for robust privacy.

171. Discuss the ethical challenges of deploying AI surveillance in public spaces.
Answer: AI surveillance may infringe on privacy and civil liberties. MCA graduates should advocate for transparency, consent-based deployment, and strict oversight to prevent misuse.

172. Explain how to ensure fault-tolerant design in critical embedded systems.
Answer: Fault-tolerant embedded systems require redundancy and error detection mechanisms. MCA graduates should implement watchdog timers, robust firmware updates, and hardware redundancy to maintain reliability.

173. Analyze how software engineers can manage API rate limiting for fair usage.
Answer: API rate limiting prevents abuse and ensures equitable access. MCA graduates should design throttling mechanisms and communicate usage policies to clients to avoid service disruption.

174. Discuss ethical concerns in developing apps that track user mental health patterns.
Answer: Mental health apps handle sensitive data and require strict confidentiality. MCA graduates should use anonymization, provide clear consent mechanisms, and avoid sharing data with third parties without user approval.

175. Explain how to optimize mobile applications for low-bandwidth networks.
Answer: Optimizing for low-bandwidth ensures usability in areas with poor connectivity. MCA graduates should minimize data usage, implement compression techniques, and allow offline functionalities to enhance user experience.

Chapter 7: Most Asked Questions Part-B

1. Analyze a situation where an Agile development team is struggling to deliver consistent increments. What steps should the project manager take?

Answer: In such a case, the project manager should first identify bottlenecks by conducting a retrospective meeting. Common issues include unclear requirements, unrealistic sprint goals, or insufficient team collaboration. Introducing daily standups, refining the backlog, and ensuring cross-functional team support can improve efficiency. MCA graduates should understand Agile principles like iterative development and prioritize communication and incremental delivery to resolve such challenges.

2. Discuss how a software engineer should handle a client requesting features that compromise system security.

Answer: When a client requests features that weaken security, such as storing passwords in plaintext, the engineer must explain potential risks, including data breaches and legal repercussions. MCA graduates should propose secure alternatives, like encrypted storage and two-factor authentication, while documenting these discussions to protect themselves ethically and professionally.

3. Explain how software engineers can handle scope creep in long-term projects.

Answer: Scope creep happens when additional features are introduced without adjusting resources or timelines. MCA graduates should manage this by implementing change control processes, documenting all requirements, and communicating the impact of changes on cost and schedule. Regular stakeholder meetings help align expectations and prevent uncontrolled expansions.

4. Analyze the challenges of integrating open-source components into a proprietary system.

Answer: Integrating open-source components can introduce licensing conflicts, security vulnerabilities, and compatibility issues. MCA graduates should carefully evaluate licenses (e.g., GPL vs MIT), perform security audits, and ensure proper documentation to mitigate risks while leveraging the benefits of open-source tools.

5. Discuss ethical responsibilities in software development when working with sensitive user data.

Answer: Handling sensitive user data, such as medical or financial information, requires adherence to data protection laws and ethical practices. MCA graduates must implement encryption, minimize data collection, and ensure user consent. Transparency about data usage builds trust and prevents legal consequences under laws like GDPR.

6. Explain how software engineers should handle tight deadlines without compromising quality.

Answer: Tight deadlines often lead to shortcuts and technical debt. MCA graduates should prioritize features using techniques like MoSCoW (Must have, Should have, Could have, Won't have), advocate realistic timelines, and use automation tools for testing and deployment. Clear communication with stakeholders about risks ensures sustainable delivery.

7. Discuss how to manage conflicts in software development teams during critical project phases.

Answer: Team conflicts can derail projects if not addressed promptly. MCA graduates should foster open communication, mediate impartially, and focus on shared project goals. Techniques like peer programming and regular feedback sessions help resolve misunderstandings and strengthen collaboration.

8. Evaluate the role of DevOps in reducing software deployment failures.

Answer: DevOps integrates development and operations to automate deployments and streamline workflows. MCA graduates should adopt practices like continuous integration/continuous deployment (CI/CD), infrastructure as code, and monitoring tools to reduce deployment errors and ensure smoother releases.

9. Explain how a software engineer should approach redesigning a legacy system without disrupting current users.

Answer: Redesigning legacy systems requires careful planning. MCA graduates should adopt a phased migration strategy, use backward compatibility techniques, and communicate changes to users. Parallel operation of old and new systems ensures minimal disruption during the transition.

10. Discuss how Agile methodologies handle changing client requirements effectively.

Answer: Agile supports changing requirements through iterative development, regular feedback loops, and flexible planning. MCA graduates should work closely with clients during sprint reviews, maintain a prioritized backlog, and embrace change as part of the process instead of resisting it.

11. Analyze a situation where a software prototype created false user expectations. How can this be avoided?
Answer: Prototypes sometimes appear more complete than they are, leading users to assume the system is production-ready. MCA graduates should clearly communicate the prototype's purpose, limitations, and scope. Using low-fidelity prototypes early on can also prevent unrealistic expectations.

12. Explain the importance of risk mitigation strategies in cloud-based software projects.
Answer: Cloud-based projects face risks like vendor lock-in, data breaches, and downtime. MCA graduates should mitigate these by designing multi-cloud strategies, implementing robust encryption, and ensuring compliance with privacy laws to build resilient and secure systems.

13. Discuss how software engineers should handle requests for unethical features in applications.
Answer: If a client requests features like user tracking without consent or discriminatory algorithms, MCA graduates must refuse politely, explaining the ethical and legal risks. They should suggest ethical alternatives and document their stance to protect their professional integrity.

14. Evaluate the role of software testing automation in large-scale projects.
Answer: Automation accelerates testing, improves accuracy, and reduces human error in large projects. MCA graduates should use tools like Selenium for functional testing and JMeter for performance testing to achieve faster, more reliable releases without compromising quality.

15. Explain how software engineers can design fault-tolerant systems for critical applications.
Answer: Fault tolerance ensures systems continue functioning despite failures. MCA graduates should implement redundancy, failover mechanisms, and error recovery techniques to design robust systems for critical domains like healthcare, banking, and transportation.

16. Discuss how to maintain software quality when working with globally distributed teams.
Answer: Global teams face challenges like time zone differences and communication gaps. MCA graduates should use collaboration tools, establish clear coding standards, and adopt asynchronous workflows to maintain consistency and quality across distributed teams.

17. Analyze the impact of poor documentation on software maintenance.
Answer: Poor documentation hinders understanding, increases maintenance time, and leads to errors. MCA graduates should maintain updated, clear documentation to support new developers and ensure smooth software evolution.

18. Explain how engineers can ensure security compliance in e-commerce applications.
Answer: Security compliance involves adhering to standards like PCI DSS for payment systems. MCA graduates should implement SSL encryption, secure APIs, and regular vulnerability scans to protect user data and prevent financial fraud.

19. Discuss the ethical implications of AI algorithms making decisions in hiring software.
Answer: AI hiring systems risk perpetuating biases if trained on flawed data. MCA graduates must ensure fairness audits, provide human oversight, and comply with employment laws to prevent discrimination and uphold ethical standards.

20. Evaluate the importance of software scalability in mobile applications.
Answer: Scalability ensures mobile apps handle increasing users and data without performance issues. MCA graduates should use load balancing, database optimization, and caching techniques to design apps that perform efficiently even under heavy loads.

21. Explain how software engineers can prevent vendor lock-in in cloud environments.

Answer: Vendor lock-in occurs when migrating away from a cloud provider becomes difficult. MCA graduates should design systems with open standards, use containerization (e.g., Docker), and adopt multi-cloud strategies to maintain flexibility.

22. Discuss how to balance innovation with ethical concerns in software development.
Answer: While innovation drives progress, it may introduce ethical risks like privacy invasion. MCA graduates should apply ethical design principles, conduct impact assessments, and prioritize user well-being alongside technical advancement.

23. Analyze a situation where a software bug caused financial loss. What lessons can engineers learn?
Answer: High-profile bugs like those in banking apps highlight the need for rigorous testing and code reviews. MCA graduates should adopt robust quality assurance practices and implement monitoring systems to detect and address issues early.

24. Explain how to manage cultural diversity in international software development projects.
Answer: Cultural diversity brings both challenges and strengths. MCA graduates should promote inclusive communication, respect different work styles, and leverage diverse perspectives to enhance creativity and problem-solving in global teams.

25. Discuss the role of user feedback in iterative software development cycles.
Answer: User feedback ensures software evolves to meet real-world needs. MCA graduates should collect feedback through surveys, beta testing, and analytics, integrating it into iterative cycles to enhance user satisfaction and product relevance.

26. Analyze how poor risk management can lead to software project failure.
Answer: Poor risk management causes unforeseen challenges like budget overruns, delays, and system vulnerabilities. For example, ignoring security risks can result in data breaches, damaging user trust and leading to legal issues. MCA graduates should learn to identify, prioritize, and mitigate risks early using tools like risk registers and contingency plans to avoid such failures and ensure project stability.

27. Discuss how to handle ethical dilemmas when a client requests deceptive UX design (dark patterns).
Answer: Dark patterns manipulate users into actions they might not intend, like accidental subscriptions. MCA graduates should reject such unethical practices, explain the long-term damage to user trust, and propose user-centric design alternatives that comply with ethical guidelines and consumer protection laws.

28. Explain the importance of continuous monitoring in large-scale distributed systems.
Answer: Continuous monitoring detects anomalies, performance bottlenecks, and security breaches in real-time. MCA graduates should implement tools like Prometheus and Grafana to ensure high availability and quick incident response, especially in systems serving millions of users globally.

29. Analyze the role of version control systems in preventing code conflicts in large teams.
Answer: Version control systems like Git manage changes, enabling multiple developers to collaborate without overwriting each other's work. MCA graduates should use branching strategies and pull requests to streamline teamwork and prevent integration conflicts in complex projects.

30. Discuss the ethical concerns of collecting behavioral data in educational apps.
Answer: While behavioral data helps personalize learning, excessive collection raises privacy issues. MCA graduates should implement data minimization, anonymization, and obtain parental consent where applicable to ensure ethical and legal compliance in handling sensitive student data.

31. Explain how to refactor legacy code without introducing new defects.
Answer: Refactoring improves code structure but risks breaking functionality. MCA graduates should follow a test-driven development (TDD) approach, write comprehensive unit tests, and apply small, incremental changes with continuous validation to ensure stability during refactoring.

32. Discuss the impact of cultural and time-zone differences in global Agile teams.

Answer: Distributed Agile teams may face challenges in coordination and communication. MCA graduates should schedule overlapping work hours, use collaboration tools like Slack or Jira, and promote cultural sensitivity training to enhance team synergy and productivity.

33. Analyze how technical debt affects software scalability.
Answer: Accumulated technical debt makes scaling difficult due to poor code quality, rigid architectures, and hidden defects. MCA graduates should prioritize debt reduction through refactoring, modular design, and regular code reviews to maintain scalability as user demand grows.

34. Explain how to design secure APIs for financial software applications.
Answer: Secure APIs protect sensitive data and prevent attacks. MCA graduates should use HTTPS, OAuth 2.0 for authentication, input validation, and rate limiting to ensure robust API security in financial systems where data breaches can have severe consequences.

35. Discuss the ethical implications of algorithmic bias in facial recognition systems.
Answer: Algorithmic bias in facial recognition can lead to discrimination and wrongful identification. MCA graduates should ensure diverse, representative training datasets and conduct fairness audits to create systems that comply with ethical standards and anti-discrimination laws.

36. Explain how software engineers can manage feature prioritization in time-constrained projects.
Answer: Feature prioritization ensures critical functionalities are delivered first. MCA graduates can use prioritization techniques like MoSCoW and involve stakeholders in backlog grooming sessions to align features with business goals under tight deadlines.

37. Discuss the challenges of migrating monolithic applications to microservices architecture.
Answer: Migrating to microservices involves challenges like data consistency, service orchestration, and increased deployment complexity. MCA graduates should adopt strategies like the strangler pattern and containerization (e.g., Docker) to gradually transition without disrupting operations.

38. Analyze how insufficient software testing impacts user trust and retention.
Answer: Poor testing leads to buggy releases, frustrating users and eroding trust. MCA graduates should design comprehensive test plans, use automated testing tools, and prioritize user experience to deliver reliable systems that retain users over time.

39. Explain how software engineers can prevent data breaches in healthcare systems.
Answer: Healthcare systems require strict compliance with privacy regulations like HIPAA. MCA graduates should use encryption, secure authentication, and regular security audits to protect sensitive medical data and prevent breaches.

40. Discuss the ethical responsibilities of developers in ensuring accessibility for users with disabilities.
Answer: Developers must create inclusive systems that comply with accessibility standards like WCAG. MCA graduates should design features like screen reader support, keyboard navigation, and appropriate color contrasts to ensure equitable access for all users.

41. Explain how to balance security and usability in mobile applications.
Answer: Strong security often conflicts with user convenience. MCA graduates should design solutions like biometric authentication and secure but simple password policies to balance robust protection with seamless user experiences.

42. Discuss the role of software engineers in ensuring disaster recovery readiness.
Answer: Disaster recovery plans minimize downtime and data loss during failures. MCA graduates should implement backup strategies, design redundant systems, and perform regular drills to ensure readiness in critical software environments.

43. Analyze the implications of open APIs on software security and innovation.
Answer: Open APIs promote innovation but increase security risks if poorly designed. MCA graduates should implement authentication, authorization, and usage monitoring to balance openness with protection.

44. Explain how software engineers can optimize applications for energy efficiency.
Answer: Energy-efficient applications extend device battery life and reduce server costs. MCA graduates should minimize background processes, optimize algorithms, and leverage efficient data transmission techniques to achieve sustainability goals.

45. Discuss the challenges of testing AI-based software systems.
Answer: AI systems are non-deterministic, making testing complex. MCA graduates should use techniques like dataset validation, bias detection, and continuous learning evaluation to ensure AI reliability and ethical performance.

46. Explain how software engineers can mitigate denial-of-service (DoS) attacks on web applications.
Answer: DoS attacks overload servers, disrupting services. MCA graduates should implement rate limiting, IP filtering, and use Content Delivery Networks (CDNs) with built-in DoS protection to enhance application resilience.

47. Discuss the role of code reviews in maintaining software security and quality.
Answer: Code reviews detect vulnerabilities and enforce coding standards. MCA graduates should actively participate in peer reviews to ensure security best practices and high-quality codebases in collaborative projects.

48. Analyze how DevOps practices improve collaboration between development and operations teams.
Answer: DevOps bridges silos by fostering shared responsibilities, continuous feedback, and automation. MCA graduates should promote CI/CD pipelines, infrastructure as code, and regular team sync-ups to enhance collaboration and delivery speed.

49. Explain the importance of ethical software licenses in project development.
Answer: Ethical licenses like GPL and MIT govern how software can be used, modified, and distributed. MCA graduates should choose appropriate licenses to respect intellectual property rights and avoid legal disputes.

50. Discuss how software engineers can support digital inclusion in rural areas.
Answer: Digital inclusion requires user-friendly, low-bandwidth applications. MCA graduates should design lightweight software, provide offline functionalities, and collaborate with local communities to make technology accessible in underserved regions.

51. Analyze the ethical issues of using user data for targeted advertisements in mobile apps.
Answer: Using user data for targeted ads raises concerns about privacy, informed consent, and potential manipulation. MCA graduates must ensure compliance with data protection laws like GDPR by obtaining explicit user consent and offering opt-out options. Ethical practices include transparency about how data is used and avoiding exploitative advertising techniques, fostering trust between users and software providers.

52. Discuss how software engineers can manage system performance issues during high traffic spikes.
Answer: High traffic spikes can cause slow response times or crashes. MCA graduates should design scalable architectures with load balancers, caching strategies, and database optimization. Using cloud-based auto-scaling can help manage unexpected surges, ensuring consistent performance and user satisfaction.

53. Explain how to design software systems with disaster recovery in mind.
Answer: Disaster recovery involves planning for system failures to minimize data loss and downtime. MCA graduates should implement regular backups, redundant systems, and failover mechanisms. Designing for geographic redundancy and creating recovery playbooks ensures systems remain operational during disasters.

54. Discuss the role of ethical hacking in preventing cybercrimes.
Answer: Ethical hacking involves authorized testing of systems to identify vulnerabilities. MCA graduates should follow responsible disclosure practices, use penetration testing tools, and collaborate with organizations to strengthen defenses. This proactive approach reduces risks and ensures compliance with cybersecurity laws.

55. Analyze the challenges of integrating AI chatbots into customer service systems.

Answer: AI chatbots enhance efficiency but may misinterpret queries or lack empathy. MCA graduates should train chatbots on diverse datasets, provide fallback mechanisms to human agents, and prioritize user privacy by securing sensitive interactions.

56. Explain how to maintain quality in rapidly changing Agile projects.
Answer: Agile projects involve frequent changes that can impact quality. MCA graduates should use automated testing, continuous integration, and regular code reviews to maintain standards. Close collaboration with stakeholders ensures new requirements are implemented effectively without compromising software stability.

57. Discuss how software engineers can ensure energy-efficient software for IoT devices.
Answer: IoT devices often have limited resources. MCA graduates should optimize algorithms, reduce data transmission, and implement sleep modes to conserve energy. Designing lightweight protocols ensures prolonged device lifespans and supports environmental sustainability.

58. Analyze the ethical responsibilities of software engineers when designing persuasive technologies.
Answer: Persuasive technologies aim to influence user behavior but risk manipulation. MCA graduates should avoid dark patterns, promote transparency, and ensure designs align with user well-being. Ethical considerations involve creating systems that empower rather than exploit users.

59. Explain how to handle data breaches in software systems responsibly.
Answer: In case of a breach, immediate action includes identifying the source, containing the damage, and notifying affected users as required by law. MCA graduates should implement strong encryption, monitor systems continuously, and follow regulatory guidelines like GDPR for breach notifications.

60. Discuss how software engineers can address ethical concerns in autonomous vehicles.
Answer: Autonomous vehicles pose ethical dilemmas, such as decision-making in accidents. MCA graduates should design systems with clear ethical frameworks, implement fail-safes, and ensure compliance with safety standards to minimize risks to passengers and pedestrians.

61. Analyze the challenges of ensuring accessibility in cross-platform software applications.
Answer: Ensuring accessibility across platforms requires consistent design and compatibility with assistive technologies. MCA graduates should follow standards like WCAG, perform usability testing with diverse user groups, and use responsive design principles to create inclusive applications.

62. Explain how software engineers can prevent insider threats in organizational systems.
Answer: Insider threats stem from employees misusing access privileges. MCA graduates should design systems with role-based access controls, activity monitoring, and anomaly detection tools to prevent unauthorized actions and protect sensitive data.

63. Discuss how to balance feature richness and simplicity in software design.
Answer: Adding too many features can overwhelm users, while too few may limit utility. MCA graduates should focus on core functionalities, use user-centered design approaches, and employ iterative feedback to balance richness with simplicity.

64. Analyze how software engineers can reduce bias in AI recruitment tools.
Answer: Bias in AI recruitment tools can perpetuate discrimination. MCA graduates should use diverse training datasets, audit algorithms for fairness, and ensure human oversight in hiring decisions to create equitable systems.

65. Explain how DevOps practices improve software deployment cycles.
Answer: DevOps integrates development and operations through automation and collaboration. MCA graduates should implement CI/CD pipelines, infrastructure as code, and monitoring tools to reduce deployment times, improve reliability, and enable faster feedback loops.

66. Discuss the ethical considerations in designing software for surveillance purposes.

Answer: Surveillance software risks infringing privacy and civil liberties. MCA graduates should implement strict access controls, anonymize data where possible, and comply with legal frameworks to ensure ethical use while safeguarding public trust.

67. Explain how software engineers can design systems for high fault tolerance in critical applications.
Answer: Critical applications require continuous availability. MCA graduates should implement redundancy, distributed architectures, and robust error-handling mechanisms to achieve fault tolerance and minimize downtime during failures.

68. Discuss the role of code optimization in enhancing software performance.
Answer: Code optimization improves efficiency and reduces resource usage. MCA graduates should profile applications, eliminate bottlenecks, and use efficient algorithms to enhance performance, especially in systems with real-time requirements.

69. Analyze how software engineers can promote open standards for interoperability.
Answer: Open standards ensure systems can communicate and integrate easily. MCA graduates should advocate for APIs, standardized protocols, and avoid vendor lock-in to promote interoperability and long-term system flexibility.

70. Explain how software engineers can ensure compliance with global data privacy regulations.
Answer: Global regulations like GDPR and CCPA require robust data protection measures. MCA graduates should design systems with privacy by design, implement user consent mechanisms, and provide tools for data portability and deletion to ensure compliance.

71. Discuss how software engineers can implement ethical AI in decision-making systems.
Answer: Ethical AI avoids bias and promotes transparency. MCA graduates should use explainable AI models, involve diverse stakeholders, and establish accountability mechanisms to ensure decisions align with ethical principles and societal values.

72. Explain how to manage version compatibility in software updates for mobile applications.
Answer: Version compatibility ensures updates don't break existing functionalities. MCA graduates should maintain backward compatibility, test on multiple devices, and provide clear update notes to users for a seamless experience.

73. Analyze how software engineers can support sustainable software development practices.
Answer: Sustainable practices include optimizing for energy efficiency, reducing server loads, and encouraging code reuse. MCA graduates should design lightweight systems and consider environmental impacts during development and deployment.

74. Discuss the ethical challenges of implementing persuasive notifications in mobile apps.
Answer: Persuasive notifications can keep users engaged but risk causing addiction or stress. MCA graduates should provide meaningful, non-intrusive alerts and allow users to control notification preferences to ensure ethical design.

75. Explain how software engineers can secure APIs against common attacks.
Answer: APIs are vulnerable to threats like injection attacks and data leaks. MCA graduates should secure APIs using authentication (e.g., OAuth), input validation, rate limiting, and regular security audits to prevent exploitation and maintain system integrity.

76. Discuss how software engineers can handle ethical issues when designing addictive features in social media apps.
Answer: Social media apps often use design elements like endless scrolling to maximize user engagement, but such features can lead to addictive behaviors. MCA graduates should evaluate the ethical implications and consider designing systems that promote healthy usage, such as screen time reminders or customizable notification settings. Balancing business goals with user well-being ensures ethical and sustainable product development.

77. Explain how software engineers can prevent SQL injection attacks in web applications.
Answer: SQL injection occurs when user inputs are not properly sanitized, allowing attackers to manipulate database queries. MCA graduates should use prepared statements, parameterized queries, and input validation techniques to

secure web applications. Regular security audits and adherence to OWASP guidelines further strengthen defenses against such attacks.

78. Analyze how software engineers can ensure fairness in algorithmic decision-making systems.
Answer: Algorithms may unintentionally favor certain groups if trained on biased data. MCA graduates should use diverse datasets, conduct fairness assessments, and implement explainable AI (XAI) techniques to promote transparency. Ethical practices involve enabling human oversight to correct biased outcomes and ensure equitable decisions.

79. Discuss the importance of load testing for large-scale e-commerce platforms.
Answer: Load testing simulates high user traffic to assess how an application performs under stress. MCA graduates should use tools like Apache JMeter to identify bottlenecks and optimize system components. Proper load testing ensures e-commerce platforms remain responsive and reliable during peak events like sales.

80. Explain how software engineers can secure sensitive data in mobile health applications.
Answer: Mobile health apps handle critical personal data. MCA graduates should apply encryption for data at rest and in transit, implement secure authentication methods like biometrics, and comply with healthcare regulations like HIPAA. Ethical practices require obtaining explicit user consent for data collection and usage.

81. Discuss the challenges of maintaining software quality in rapid release cycles.
Answer: Rapid releases, common in Agile and DevOps, risk introducing defects due to reduced testing time. MCA graduates should adopt automated testing, continuous integration, and robust code review practices to maintain quality without slowing delivery.

82. Explain how software engineers can mitigate risks in outsourcing software development.
Answer: Outsourcing introduces risks like communication barriers, quality inconsistencies, and data breaches. MCA graduates should establish clear contracts, define detailed specifications, and use secure collaboration tools. Regular monitoring and quality checks ensure successful outsourcing partnerships.

83. Analyze how software engineers can prevent misuse of facial recognition technology.
Answer: Facial recognition can compromise privacy if used irresponsibly. MCA graduates should design systems with strict consent requirements, data anonymization, and purpose limitation. Compliance with privacy laws like GDPR is crucial to prevent misuse and protect user rights.

84. Discuss the role of ethical guidelines in developing autonomous drones for delivery services.
Answer: Autonomous drones raise safety and privacy concerns. MCA graduates should follow ethical design principles, ensuring drones avoid private property, comply with aviation laws, and include fail-safe mechanisms. Transparent communication with the public builds trust in such technologies.

85. Explain how software engineers can design systems for multilingual support.
Answer: Multilingual support broadens user reach and improves inclusivity. MCA graduates should use Unicode standards, separate language resources from core logic, and provide localization frameworks. Testing with native speakers ensures cultural appropriateness and usability.

86. Discuss how to ensure software compliance with international intellectual property (IP) laws.
Answer: Software IP compliance involves respecting copyrights, patents, and licenses globally. MCA graduates should track third-party components, verify licensing terms, and avoid using pirated tools. Proper documentation and audits help organizations avoid legal disputes.

87. Analyze how software engineers can secure IoT ecosystems against cyber threats.
Answer: IoT devices often lack robust security, making them vulnerable. MCA graduates should design secure communication protocols, enforce strong authentication, and implement regular firmware updates to protect IoT systems from cyberattacks.

88. Explain how software engineers can balance user personalization and data privacy in applications.

Answer: Personalization enhances user experience but risks violating privacy if data is misused. MCA graduates should implement anonymization techniques, transparent privacy policies, and allow users to control how their data is used. Compliance with regulations ensures ethical personalization.

89. Discuss the challenges of software scalability in microservices architectures.
Answer: Microservices offer scalability by allowing independent scaling of components, but they introduce complexities like inter-service communication and data consistency. MCA graduates should use API gateways, message queues, and distributed transaction management to handle these challenges effectively.

90. Explain the role of software engineers in ensuring ethical AI usage in surveillance systems.
Answer: AI-powered surveillance can lead to mass monitoring and rights violations. MCA graduates must implement ethical safeguards like purpose limitation, transparency, and oversight mechanisms to ensure systems align with privacy laws and human rights standards.

91. Discuss the ethical responsibilities of software engineers in open-source contributions.
Answer: Open-source contributions require adherence to community guidelines and respect for intellectual property. MCA graduates should submit high-quality, well-documented code, avoid introducing malicious elements, and engage constructively with the community to uphold ethical standards.

92. Analyze the importance of performance optimization in real-time applications.
Answer: Real-time applications require low latency and high responsiveness. MCA graduates should optimize algorithms, use efficient data structures, and leverage hardware acceleration to ensure real-time performance, especially in domains like gaming and healthcare monitoring.

93. Explain how software engineers can prevent phishing attacks in enterprise systems.
Answer: Phishing exploits user trust to steal credentials. MCA graduates should design systems with multi-factor authentication, email filters, and user awareness training to reduce phishing risks and protect organizational assets.

94. Discuss the challenges of maintaining legacy systems while integrating modern technologies.
Answer: Legacy systems often use outdated technologies incompatible with modern tools. MCA graduates should adopt hybrid approaches, use APIs for integration, and plan gradual migrations to ensure business continuity without disrupting operations.

95. Explain how software engineers can design energy-efficient server systems for large enterprises.
Answer: Energy efficiency reduces costs and environmental impact. MCA graduates should optimize server workloads, use virtualization, and implement dynamic scaling to manage resource consumption effectively in enterprise systems.

96. Discuss how software engineers can ensure ethical use of user location data in ride-sharing apps.
Answer: Location data is sensitive and prone to misuse. MCA graduates should obtain explicit consent, limit data retention, and anonymize user locations to balance functionality with privacy in ride-sharing applications.

97. Analyze how continuous delivery practices improve software reliability.
Answer: Continuous delivery automates software deployment, reducing human errors and enabling quick updates. MCA graduates should implement CI/CD pipelines, automated tests, and rollback mechanisms to ensure high reliability and faster release cycles.

98. Explain the role of software engineers in developing inclusive educational technologies.
Answer: Inclusive educational technologies cater to diverse learners, including those with disabilities. MCA graduates should design systems with accessibility features like text-to-speech, adaptive interfaces, and support for multiple learning styles.

99. Discuss how software engineers can prevent overfitting in AI models.
Answer: Overfitting occurs when AI models perform well on training data but poorly on new data. MCA graduates should use techniques like cross-validation, regularization, and data augmentation to build robust, generalizable models.

100. Explain how software engineers can support ethical innovation in blockchain applications.
Answer: Blockchain applications require transparency and fairness. MCA graduates should ensure smart contracts are secure, design systems that minimize energy consumption, and comply with financial regulations to promote ethical blockchain innovation.

101. Discuss how software engineers can ensure data integrity in financial applications.
Answer: Data integrity in financial systems is critical to prevent loss, fraud, and regulatory violations. MCA graduates should implement checksums, transaction logs, and validation rules to ensure accurate data processing. Techniques like ACID properties in databases and encryption during data transmission further protect integrity. Regular audits and automated reconciliation processes help maintain trust and compliance in financial applications.

102. Explain how to handle ethical challenges in AI-based predictive policing systems.
Answer: Predictive policing may reinforce societal biases if AI is trained on flawed historical data. MCA graduates should apply fairness-aware algorithms, conduct bias audits, and involve diverse stakeholders in system design. Ethical safeguards like transparency and accountability frameworks ensure the technology supports justice without discrimination.

103. Analyze how software engineers can manage resource constraints in embedded systems development.
Answer: Embedded systems often operate under strict memory, processing, and energy constraints. MCA graduates should write efficient code, use lightweight operating systems, and optimize hardware-software integration. Proper resource management ensures systems remain reliable, especially in critical applications like medical devices or automotive controls.

104. Discuss how software engineers can ensure GDPR compliance in e-commerce platforms.
Answer: GDPR mandates strict user privacy controls, including data minimization, explicit consent, and the right to be forgotten. MCA graduates should design systems with privacy-by-design principles, provide clear privacy policies, and implement tools for data export and deletion to meet regulatory standards.

105. Explain how software engineers can prevent cascading failures in distributed systems.
Answer: Cascading failures occur when one component's failure triggers others. MCA graduates should design with circuit breakers, implement redundancy, and use monitoring tools to detect and isolate faults early. Techniques like graceful degradation ensure systems continue operating despite localized issues.

106. Discuss ethical considerations when developing persuasive health apps.
Answer: Persuasive health apps encourage positive habits but risk exploiting users' vulnerabilities. MCA graduates should prioritize user autonomy, provide transparent explanations of recommendations, and avoid creating pressure or guilt. Ethical designs focus on empowering users rather than manipulating them.

107. Analyze how software engineers can manage interoperability challenges in heterogeneous systems.
Answer: Interoperability requires seamless communication between diverse systems. MCA graduates should use open standards, APIs, and middleware solutions to bridge differences. Proper documentation and adherence to protocols like REST or SOAP ensure smooth integration in complex environments.

108. Explain how to balance innovation and security in IoT product development.
Answer: IoT innovation often prioritizes features, leaving security as an afterthought. MCA graduates should integrate security from the start using secure boot, encryption, and access controls. Balancing both ensures products are functional, user-friendly, and protected from cyber threats.

109. Discuss the role of software engineers in preventing intellectual property theft in software projects.
Answer: Protecting intellectual property (IP) involves securing source code, using obfuscation, and enforcing licensing agreements. MCA graduates should implement access controls, monitor repositories, and educate teams about IP laws to prevent accidental or intentional IP theft.

110. Explain how to design fault-tolerant cloud applications for high availability.

Answer: High availability ensures minimal downtime in cloud systems. MCA graduates should use load balancers, auto-scaling, and multi-region deployments to achieve resilience. Designing with distributed architectures and regular failover testing prepares systems for unexpected disruptions.

111. Discuss how software engineers can ensure ethical practices in social media algorithm design.
Answer: Social media algorithms can create echo chambers or promote harmful content. MCA graduates should focus on transparency, offer users control over recommendations, and prioritize content moderation strategies to promote ethical engagement.

112. Analyze the challenges of maintaining backward compatibility in software updates.
Answer: Backward compatibility ensures older systems continue functioning with new updates. MCA graduates should maintain APIs, use versioning, and conduct regression testing to avoid breaking existing functionalities while enabling innovation.

113. Explain how software engineers can address latency issues in real-time systems.
Answer: Low latency is vital for real-time systems like gaming or autonomous vehicles. MCA graduates should optimize algorithms, reduce network hops, and use edge computing to minimize delays and ensure timely responses.

114. Discuss ethical concerns in AI-powered hiring systems used by enterprises.
Answer: AI hiring tools risk perpetuating bias and lack transparency in decision-making. MCA graduates must implement fairness testing, provide explainability, and ensure human oversight to maintain ethical recruitment practices and comply with anti-discrimination laws.

115. Explain how software engineers can secure sensitive APIs in fintech applications.
Answer: Fintech APIs handle critical transactions and user data. MCA graduates should use API gateways, implement OAuth 2.0 authentication, rate limiting, and monitor for unusual activities to protect APIs from threats like data leaks or fraud.

116. Analyze how software engineers can mitigate risks of single points of failure in large systems.
Answer: Single points of failure (SPOF) can bring down entire systems. MCA graduates should design redundancy, use distributed architectures, and implement failover mechanisms to eliminate SPOFs and ensure system resilience.

117. Discuss the role of ethical responsibility in designing addictive gaming features.
Answer: Addictive gaming features like loot boxes and reward cycles can harm users. MCA graduates should design responsibly, avoiding manipulative mechanics and providing tools for users to manage their gaming habits and screen time.

118. Explain how to manage software scalability for global video streaming platforms.
Answer: Scalability for video streaming requires content delivery networks (CDNs), adaptive bitrate streaming, and distributed databases. MCA graduates should design systems to handle millions of concurrent users while maintaining quality and reducing latency worldwide.

119. Discuss how software engineers can ensure secure DevOps pipelines.
Answer: Securing DevOps pipelines involves protecting code repositories, using signed builds, and implementing access controls. MCA graduates should integrate security testing into CI/CD workflows to prevent vulnerabilities from reaching production environments.

120. Explain how software engineers can design multi-tenant architectures for SaaS applications.
Answer: Multi-tenant architectures allow multiple customers to share infrastructure securely. MCA graduates should use tenant isolation, data partitioning, and robust access controls to ensure data security and scalability in SaaS systems.

121. Analyze how software engineers can prevent API abuse in public-facing applications.
Answer: API abuse can lead to denial-of-service or data scraping attacks. MCA graduates should use API keys, rate limiting, and behavioral analytics to detect and prevent misuse while maintaining service availability for legitimate users.

122. Discuss the importance of software observability in complex distributed systems.
Answer: Observability helps teams understand system behavior through metrics, logs, and traces. MCA graduates should implement observability tools like Prometheus and Grafana to monitor performance and troubleshoot issues proactively.

123. Explain how software engineers can ethically manage user data in fitness tracking applications.
Answer: Fitness apps collect sensitive health data. MCA graduates should use anonymization, obtain user consent, and comply with privacy regulations like GDPR to protect user data and maintain trust.

124. Discuss the challenges of software maintenance in AI-powered systems.
Answer: AI systems require continuous retraining and monitoring for model drift. MCA graduates should implement feedback loops, maintain datasets, and ensure explainability to support effective and ethical maintenance of AI systems.

125. Explain how software engineers can prevent over-engineering in software design.
Answer: Over-engineering adds unnecessary complexity, increasing costs and maintenance efforts. MCA graduates should focus on simplicity, prioritize user needs, and adopt iterative development to avoid building excessive features that provide little value.

126. Discuss how software engineers can design privacy-first social networking applications.
Answer: Privacy-first social networking apps prioritize user data protection. MCA graduates should incorporate end-to-end encryption, allow granular privacy controls for posts, and avoid excessive data collection. Systems should have transparent data usage policies and support anonymous interactions where possible. Compliance with global privacy laws like GDPR ensures ethical practices while fostering user trust in social networking environments.

127. Explain the role of software engineers in minimizing algorithmic bias in loan approval systems.
Answer: Bias in loan systems can discriminate against certain groups due to flawed training data. MCA graduates should ensure datasets are diverse, implement fairness-aware algorithms, and conduct bias audits. Collaborating with financial and legal experts helps align systems with ethical and regulatory standards to deliver equitable outcomes.

128. Analyze how to design software for disaster-resilient supply chain management systems.
Answer: Supply chains are vulnerable to disruptions from natural disasters. MCA graduates should design systems with real-time tracking, predictive analytics, and multi-location data backups. Incorporating AI for risk analysis and cloud-based solutions enhances resilience and supports quick recovery during crises.

129. Discuss how software engineers can ethically manage location tracking in mobile applications.
Answer: Location tracking enhances app features but raises privacy concerns. MCA graduates should adopt opt-in mechanisms, limit location data to essential functions, and allow users to disable tracking. Transparent notifications and data anonymization ensure ethical and legal compliance while respecting user autonomy.

130. Explain how software engineers can handle version conflicts in collaborative coding platforms.
Answer: Version conflicts arise when multiple developers edit the same codebase. MCA graduates should use version control systems like Git with branching strategies (e.g., Gitflow) and conduct frequent merges. Code review processes and CI tools help resolve conflicts proactively in collaborative environments.

131. Analyze the ethical implications of using AI in social media content moderation.
Answer: AI moderation systems can mislabel or censor legitimate content. MCA graduates should ensure transparency, involve human oversight for sensitive cases, and avoid bias in training data. Designing systems with explainable AI (XAI) helps build fairness and user trust.

132. Discuss how software engineers can design fault-tolerant systems for financial transactions.
Answer: Financial systems require high reliability. MCA graduates should use redundant databases, transaction logs, and ACID-compliant systems to prevent data loss. Implementing failover mechanisms and real-time monitoring ensures fault tolerance and continuous availability for critical transactions.

133. Explain how software engineers can implement secure authentication in e-learning platforms.
Answer: Secure authentication prevents unauthorized access to sensitive student data. MCA graduates should use multi-factor authentication (MFA), OAuth protocols, and strong password policies. Encryption of credentials and session management further strengthens security in e-learning environments.

134. Analyze how to balance innovation and ethical constraints in smart home devices.
Answer: Smart home devices offer convenience but may intrude on privacy. MCA graduates should implement strict data encryption, allow users control over collected data, and design systems with clear consent mechanisms to ethically balance innovation and user rights.

135. Discuss how software engineers can manage software regressions in continuous delivery pipelines.
Answer: Software regressions reintroduce old bugs in new releases. MCA graduates should implement automated regression tests, version control rollbacks, and monitoring tools to detect and address issues promptly within CI/CD workflows.

136. Explain how software engineers can support inclusivity in gaming applications.
Answer: Inclusivity in games involves designing for diverse players. MCA graduates should include customizable avatars, support accessibility features like subtitles and color-blind modes, and ensure content is culturally sensitive to appeal to a global audience.

137. Analyze the importance of ethical considerations in wearable health tracking devices.
Answer: Wearable devices collect sensitive health data that could be misused. MCA graduates must prioritize encryption, anonymize data before analysis, and obtain explicit user consent. Compliance with regulations like HIPAA ensures ethical and legal integrity in health tech development.

138. Discuss how software engineers can secure APIs in smart city applications.
Answer: Smart city APIs handle critical data on traffic, utilities, and public services. MCA graduates should use token-based authentication, rate limiting, and encrypted communication channels. Regular API security audits prevent breaches and maintain system integrity.

139. Explain how software engineers can design efficient caching strategies for high-traffic websites.
Answer: Caching reduces server load and speeds up responses. MCA graduates should use techniques like content delivery networks (CDNs), in-memory caches (Redis), and cache invalidation policies to balance freshness and performance for high-traffic websites.

140. Analyze the challenges of designing software for autonomous delivery robots.
Answer: Autonomous delivery robots face challenges like obstacle detection and real-time decision-making. MCA graduates should implement sensor fusion, AI navigation systems, and robust error-handling mechanisms to ensure safety and reliability in dynamic environments.

141. Discuss the ethical use of artificial intelligence in predictive hiring tools.
Answer: Predictive hiring tools risk bias and lack transparency. MCA graduates should audit AI models for fairness, provide explainability to users, and ensure final decisions involve human judgment to maintain ethical hiring practices.

142. Explain how software engineers can prevent session hijacking in web applications.
Answer: Session hijacking compromises user sessions. MCA graduates should use secure cookies, enable HTTPS, implement session timeouts, and regenerate session IDs upon login to protect users from unauthorized access.

143. Discuss the role of observability in maintaining distributed cloud systems.
Answer: Observability provides insights into system behavior using logs, metrics, and traces. MCA graduates should implement observability frameworks to monitor distributed systems, detect anomalies, and resolve issues proactively in cloud environments.

144. Analyze the ethical concerns of implementing surveillance features in parental control software.
Answer: Parental control software must balance child safety and privacy. MCA graduates should design features that avoid over-monitoring, offer transparency to both parents and children, and comply with privacy laws like COPPA.

145. Explain how software engineers can secure data storage in serverless applications.
Answer: Serverless apps rely on third-party storage, increasing exposure. MCA graduates should use encrypted storage solutions, enforce role-based access controls, and regularly rotate access keys to secure sensitive data.

146. Discuss how to design responsive UI/UX for cross-platform software.
Answer: Responsive designs adapt to various screen sizes and devices. MCA graduates should use flexible layouts, media queries, and scalable vector graphics (SVGs) to ensure consistent user experiences across platforms.

147. Analyze how software engineers can ensure ethical deployment of AI in fraud detection systems.
Answer: Fraud detection systems can unfairly flag legitimate transactions. MCA graduates should fine-tune models to minimize false positives, implement human review for edge cases, and ensure transparency in decision-making to avoid user frustration.

148. Explain how software engineers can secure blockchain networks against double-spending attacks.
Answer: Double-spending compromises trust in blockchain systems. MCA graduates should design networks with robust consensus mechanisms (e.g., proof-of-work or proof-of-stake) and monitor transactions for anomalies to prevent such attacks.

149. Discuss the role of ethical responsibility in designing AR experiences for public spaces.
Answer: AR in public spaces may disrupt social interactions or privacy. MCA graduates should design opt-in systems, avoid intrusive content, and consider the cultural context to ensure ethical deployment.

150. Explain how software engineers can implement role-based access control (RBAC) in enterprise systems.
Answer: RBAC assigns permissions based on user roles, minimizing unauthorized access. MCA graduates should design granular roles, enforce least-privilege principles, and audit access rights regularly for secure enterprise systems.

151. Explain how software engineers can implement real-time analytics in large-scale e-commerce platforms.
Answer: Real-time analytics helps e-commerce platforms track user behavior, inventory, and sales trends instantly. MCA graduates should use streaming data platforms like Apache Kafka and processing engines like Apache Flink or Spark Streaming. Designing systems with scalable data pipelines and in-memory databases ensures timely insights. Implementing dashboards allows stakeholders to monitor KPIs and make informed decisions quickly during peak traffic events.

152. Discuss the ethical concerns in developing AI-powered emotional recognition systems.
Answer: Emotional recognition systems analyze facial expressions or speech to interpret emotions, but they raise privacy and accuracy concerns. MCA graduates should avoid deploying such systems in contexts where consent is unclear or misuse is possible. Ensuring transparency, securing user data, and acknowledging cultural differences in emotional expressions are vital to ethical deployment.

153. Analyze how software engineers can design secure payment gateways for mobile applications.
Answer: Payment gateways in mobile apps handle sensitive financial data. MCA graduates should implement encryption (TLS/SSL), tokenization, and PCI DSS compliance. Multi-factor authentication (MFA) and fraud detection systems further protect users. Regular security audits and adherence to best practices ensure safe and reliable payment processing.

154. Explain how to handle data consistency challenges in distributed caching systems.
Answer: Distributed caching improves performance but may cause stale data issues. MCA graduates should use cache-coherency protocols, time-to-live (TTL) policies, and write-through/write-back strategies to maintain consistency. Techniques like eventual consistency in distributed systems can balance performance with accuracy.

155. Discuss how software engineers can ensure ethical practices in designing persuasive gamification features in education apps.
Answer: Gamification boosts engagement but risks making users overly dependent on rewards. MCA graduates should prioritize educational outcomes, design non-addictive reward systems, and provide opt-out options. Ethical gamification encourages intrinsic motivation rather than manipulation.

156. Explain how software engineers can implement disaster recovery plans for multi-cloud environments.
Answer: Multi-cloud environments distribute workloads across providers for resilience. MCA graduates should design redundant architectures, use automated failover mechanisms, and maintain regular backups in geographically separated regions. Testing recovery plans ensures readiness during outages.

157. Discuss the challenges of developing software for autonomous agricultural robots.
Answer: Agricultural robots face dynamic environments with uneven terrains and weather variability. MCA graduates should integrate robust sensor systems, AI models for obstacle detection, and fault-tolerant software architectures. Remote monitoring and updates enhance reliability in critical farming operations.

158. Analyze how software engineers can secure communication in IoT medical devices.
Answer: IoT medical devices transmit sensitive health data, requiring strict security. MCA graduates should use end-to-end encryption, secure boot processes, and regular firmware updates. Compliance with regulations like HIPAA ensures ethical and legal operation.

159. Explain the role of continuous performance testing in maintaining enterprise software quality.
Answer: Continuous performance testing identifies bottlenecks and ensures scalability as systems evolve. MCA graduates should integrate tools like JMeter or Gatling into CI/CD pipelines to monitor response times and resource utilization. Proactive testing prevents performance degradation in production environments.

160. Discuss how software engineers can address ethical concerns in designing AI for content curation on news platforms.
Answer: AI-powered content curation can amplify biases or misinformation. MCA graduates should ensure algorithms provide diverse perspectives, avoid echo chambers, and allow user customization. Transparency in how content is prioritized helps build trust in news platforms.

161. Explain how software engineers can optimize mobile app performance for devices with limited resources.
Answer: Optimization ensures apps run smoothly on low-end devices. MCA graduates should use lightweight frameworks, minimize background processes, and optimize images and assets. Caching frequently accessed data and reducing API calls further improve performance.

162. Discuss how software engineers can design ethical digital assistants for vulnerable populations.
Answer: Digital assistants for seniors or children must prioritize safety and privacy. MCA graduates should include clear consent mechanisms, restrict data sharing, and design intuitive interfaces. Features like reminders and emergency alerts must be reliable and non-intrusive.

163. Analyze how to secure user identities in decentralized applications (dApps).
Answer: dApps rely on blockchain for security but require additional measures for identity management. MCA graduates should use decentralized identifiers (DIDs), multi-signature wallets, and encrypted key storage to protect user identities.

164. Explain how software engineers can design scalable video analytics systems for traffic management.
Answer: Video analytics for traffic requires processing large data streams in real-time. MCA graduates should leverage edge computing for local processing, use AI models for object detection, and design scalable cloud architectures for aggregation and analysis.

165. Discuss ethical considerations in designing AI-powered hiring chatbots.
Answer: Hiring chatbots risk introducing bias and making opaque decisions. MCA graduates should ensure diverse training datasets, provide explanations for decisions, and allow human intervention to uphold fairness and transparency.

166. Explain how software engineers can prevent unauthorized API access in fintech applications.
Answer: Preventing unauthorized API access is crucial for financial systems. MCA graduates should implement API gateways, use OAuth 2.0 for secure authorization, and monitor for anomalies. Rate limiting and IP whitelisting further strengthen API security.

167. Discuss the challenges of integrating legacy systems into modern cloud platforms.
Answer: Legacy systems may have outdated architectures and dependencies. MCA graduates should design APIs for communication, use containerization (e.g., Docker) for compatibility, and adopt a phased migration strategy to minimize disruptions.

168. Analyze how software engineers can develop sustainable software for energy monitoring systems.
Answer: Energy monitoring systems should minimize resource consumption. MCA graduates should design lightweight software, optimize algorithms for low-power hardware, and support renewable energy integration for environmentally sustainable solutions.

169. Explain how to design ethical data-sharing policies in health research applications.
Answer: Health research apps handle sensitive data requiring strict ethical oversight. MCA graduates should anonymize data, obtain explicit user consent, and comply with privacy laws like GDPR. Transparent policies ensure trust and responsible data sharing.

170. Discuss the role of software engineers in promoting green software engineering practices.
Answer: Green software engineering reduces environmental impact through efficient coding and resource use. MCA graduates should optimize algorithms, support hardware recycling, and design systems that consume less power for sustainability.

171. Explain how software engineers can secure mobile banking applications against phishing attacks.
Answer: Phishing attacks deceive users into revealing credentials. MCA graduates should design apps with multi-factor authentication, educate users with anti-phishing alerts, and use app-based verification to prevent fraud.

172. Analyze how software engineers can design ethical AI systems for autonomous vehicles.
Answer: Autonomous vehicles face ethical dilemmas like prioritizing safety in unavoidable crashes. MCA graduates should design transparent decision-making frameworks, adhere to legal standards, and involve diverse stakeholders to align AI behavior with societal ethics.

173. Discuss how software engineers can prevent ransomware attacks in enterprise systems.
Answer: Ransomware encrypts critical data for ransom. MCA graduates should enforce regular backups, use endpoint detection systems, and apply strict access controls. Security awareness training for employees reduces risks from phishing vectors.

174. Explain how software engineers can optimize software for devices with intermittent network connectivity.
Answer: Applications for such environments should use offline-first architectures, local caching, and synchronization mechanisms. MCA graduates should design lightweight protocols and minimize reliance on continuous connectivity to ensure usability.

175. Discuss ethical challenges in designing AI systems for emotion-based marketing.
Answer: Emotion-based marketing leverages user emotions for sales but risks manipulation. MCA graduates should ensure transparency, provide opt-out options, and avoid targeting vulnerable populations to maintain ethical practices.

Printed at Repro India Ltd.